Me as a baby.

Marshfield
Dreams

Me with Dad and Mom.

RALPH FLETCHER

Marshfield Dreams

When I Was a Kid

HENRY HOLT AND COMPANY ✦ NEW YORK

Henry Holt and Company, LLC
Publishers since 1866
175 Fifth Avenue
New York, New York 10010
www.HenryHoltKids.com

Henry Holt® is a registered trademark of Henry Holt and Company, LLC.
Copyright © 2005 by Ralph Fletcher
Illustrations copyright © 2005 by Esy Casey
Map illustration copyright © 2005 by Jennifer Thermes
All rights reserved.
Distributed in Canada by H. B. Fenn and Company Ltd.

Library of Congress Cataloging-in-Publication Data
Fletcher, Ralph J.
Marshfield dreams : when I was a kid / Ralph Fletcher.—1st ed.
p.   cm.
ISBN-13: 978-0-8050-7242-6
ISBN-10: 0-8050-7242-X
1. Fletcher, Ralph J.—Childhood and youth—Juvenile literature.   2.
Fletcher, Ralph J.—Homes and haunts—Massachusetts—Marshfield—
Juvenile literature.   3. Authors, American—20th century—Biography—
Juvenile literature.   4. Marshfield (Mass.)—Social life and customs—
Juvenile literature.   I. Title.
PS3556.L523Z47 2005   811'.54—dc22   [B]   2004060746

First edition—2005 / Designed by Patrick Collins
Printed in the United States of America on acid-free paper. ∞

10 9 8 7 6 5 4 3

Me with Dad and Mom again.

*This book is dedicated to my father,
my sisters and brothers,
especially Jimmy,*

*to my old best friends
Andy Hunt, Steve Fishman,
and Freddy Fletcher,*

*and to my beloved mother,
Jean Fletcher (1929–2004)*

My house on Acorn Street, Marshfield.

Marshfield
Dreams

Me, about age four or five.

Marshfield

THERE'S A TOWN called Marshfield in the state of Vermont. You can also find a Marshfield in Maine, one in Missouri, and one in Wisconsin. I grew up in Marshfield, Massachusetts. The curly part of Massachusetts that sticks out into the ocean is Cape Cod. Marshfield sits on the ocean, just above that curl.

I lived on Acorn Street in a regular house bordered by forest on two sides. Dad owned seven acres of woods in back. Across a dirt driveway we had Ale's Woods, a forest of pine trees. The pines dropped millions of needles, which gave the forest floor a nice, springy feel. Those trees were great for climbing. If I crawled out too far on a limb and fell, the soft needles cushioned my fall, so I never got hurt.

The woods held magical things. We found snake skins, real Indian arrowheads, box turtles, beehives, snake spit on tall grass. We dug up the buried trash from people who lived there many years before. We saw gravestones so old we could no longer read the names carved in them. We found all kinds of mushrooms. Some were edible, and others were poisonous toadstools. Mom said to think of them as strangers—some are good, some are bad, and since you couldn't tell the difference it was best to leave them alone. One morning in the woods I stepped into a fairy ring of mushrooms, a big circle ten feet across.

There was a tiny stream in our backyard small enough so you could step from one bank to the other. This stream flowed under the dirt driveway and formed a swamp at the edge of Ale's Woods. I loved the dank smell of that swamp and all the things that lived there: mossy logs and goggle-eyed frogs, bloodsuckers and eels and foul-smelling skunk cabbage. Half the swamp was underwater, and the other half contained thick, dense mud. It was impossible to walk through that muck without getting stuck. More than once I tried and left behind one of my sneakers, a lost sole sunk forever at the bottom of the swamp. I got in trouble for that. But today I'm glad to know that something of mine was left behind in Marsh-field.

Here is my story.

Me, age two, in a wagon.

Junior

As THE OLDEST of nine, I was named after my father and my grandfather. Some kids on Acorn Street teased me, calling: "Hey, Juuuu-nioooor!" not that I minded. I liked having the same name as my father, but it did cause confusion in the house.

Whenever Mom called out, "Ralph!" Dad and I would both answer, "Yeah?"

"No, Big Ralph!" or, "Little Ralph!" she yelled back, to clarify things. I guess that would have annoyed some people, but it didn't really bother me. Dad was tall and handsome. I bragged to my friends that my father was so cool he had three jobs: teacher, milkman, bartender. I was proud of him. I loved knowing that *Ralph* could fit us both in one snug syllable.

Me, Lainie, and Jimmy.

Statue
Age 3

BY THE TIME I was three I already had a brother, Jimmy, who was a year younger than me. My sister Elaine was a year younger than Jim. Dad worked as a traveling book salesman, and Mom took care of us when Dad was away. Dad came home on Friday nights. On Saturdays, after breakfast, the whole family would play outside.

As soon as I saw Mom and Dad coming out the

door, I'd get excited and run to the big boulder in the front yard. We were about to play my favorite game, Statue. I arranged my body in a certain pose and froze. Then I closed my eyes, waiting. My heart beat faster as they came closer.

"What's this?" Dad asked.

"It looks like a statue!" Mom said. She had Jimmy and Lainie in the stroller and pushed them closer.

"A statue of a little boy!" Dad exclaimed. "It's beautiful! It's absolutely perfect! Amazing!"

Mom knelt to touch my nose. I could feel the eyes of my whole family studying me closely. Jimmy laughed. The baby just stared.

"A little boy, carved in stone!" Mom exclaimed. "You think we could buy it?"

"Hey, look!" Dad said. "There's a price tag right here on the sleeve!"

I remained absolutely still, barely breathing, while Dad examined the invisible tag.

"How much?" Mom asked impatiently. "How much is it?"

"It's a lot—one hundred dollars!" Dad told her. "But who cares? It's worth every penny! I'd pay five hundred dollars for a statue like this! I'd pay a thousand!"

I tried hard not to smile.

"Excuse me, madam," Dad said to baby Lainie. "Is this your store? My wife and I would like to buy this statue here. A hundred dollars? Certainly. Here you go. Ten, twenty, thirty, forty, fifty, sixty, seventy, eighty, ninety, one hundred. What? Ship it? No, no thank you. We'll just put it in our car and drive it home."

He handed Lainie to Mom and picked me up. With me in his lap, stiff as a board, he sat on the boulder. Mom sat beside him. Dad pretended to turn on the car ignition.

"Drive carefully," Mom said. "We don't want the statue to get damaged."

"Don't worry," Dad replied, while turning the steering wheel. He pretended to park the car. "Here we are."

"Where should we put the statue?" Mom asked.

"I've got the perfect place for it," he said. "Right here in our front yard."

"How wonderful," Mom exclaimed. "We've got two boys, but I've always wanted another."

"Look at the detail on the face." Dad bent down to examine me closely. "It almost looks alive!"

That was my cue. Slowly, I lifted my chin and looked up, first at my father, then at my mother.

"My goodness!" they shouted. "He's alive!"

Hugs! Kisses!

"It's a real boy!" Dad exclaimed. "Would you like to live with us?"

Shyly, I nodded. With more hugs and kisses, they welcomed me into the family.

"It's a miracle," Dad kept saying. "An absolute miracle."

Jimmy and me.

Kids
Age 5

MOM HAD A BABY every year—me, Jimmy, Lainie, Tommy—boom, boom, boom, boom.

Babies needed baby food, formula, diapers, medicine. Babies were expensive, and Mom was always looking for ways to save money. We never went to the barber shop. Instead, Mom cut the boys' hair with electric clippers, shaving our heads on the back porch and sweeping the hair into the bushes afterward.

"The birds will gather your hair and use it to make their nests nice and warm," she said.

Mom gave me a whiffle haircut so short I could see my scalp when I looked in the mirror. The haircut was perfect for hot summer days, but it didn't hide the place in front where my hair jutted straight up as if being blown that way by invisible wind. No matter what I tried—water, spit, Vaseline—that hair insisted on doing exactly what it wanted.

Jimmy had a cowlick even worse than mine. Half the hair went straight up, the other half straight down, like a riptide. With Jimmy's cowlick, plus the fact that he wore glasses, I thought he looked even goofier than me.

Lainie had reddish hair that Mom cut with a pair of scissors. Lainie didn't like bugs. Once, a small ant crawled on her and she started screaming. It took Mom a long time to calm her down. After that, Jimmy nicknamed her the Screech Owl.

I mostly played with Jimmy. We were close but different. Even as a baby he would do stuff that I'd never dream of doing. One time Mom put him in his stroller and took us out for a walk. A lady came by and bent down to look at him.

"Aren't you just the most adorable thing?" she cooed.

Jimmy smiled and cooed back. But as soon as the lady turned around Jimmy stuck out his tongue at her.

Mom wanted us to be good, and I *was* good. I knew what the rules were and followed them. As the oldest, I tried to get the other kids to follow them too, but Jimmy wouldn't listen. Rules were for other people, not for him.

One night Dad and Mom got a babysitter, a high school girl more interested in talking on the telephone than taking care of us. She sent us to bed early without a snack. Mom had just bought new bedspreads that had little string fringes. Jimmy began to unravel the strings.

"You better not do that," I warned, but once Jimmy got started, there was no stopping him. He pulled all the strings out. Then he set up a system of lines and pulleys between my top bunk bed and his bed on the bottom. Lainie let him wrap a string around one of her dolls. When I pulled the string, the doll started rising slowly up to my bunk. We laughed, watching it go higher and higher. Suddenly, its eyes popped open, like it was scared stiff, and we began shrieking with such laughter that the babysitter ran upstairs to see what was going on.

Next day, when Mom found that we had pulled all the strings out of the new bedspreads, she burst into tears. That night she sent us to bed right after supper, in the middle of the summer. I thought that it was the worst punishment any kid had ever had. Not the least bit tired, I laid in bed for hours as the room slowly changed from day to night, listening to my friends outside on Acorn Street playing a wild game of Kick-the-Can without me.

Me, about age six.

The Pratts

Age 6

Wʜᴇɴ ᴛʜᴇ sɴᴏw melted in early March, Mom put the little kids in the stroller and took us outside. We played a game called Signs of Spring. Mom awarded points to any one of us who noticed buds on the bushes, a few small blades of grass, or maybe a flower named a crocus pushing up through the muddy dirt.

My world on Acorn Street seemed perfect,

complete. But certain things began to happen that made me aware of another, bigger world.

"The pope died," Mom said one morning at breakfast.

"Who's the pope?" I asked.

"He was the head of the Catholic Church," she explained. "He was the holiest man on earth."

I knew one thing for sure: The pope would go straight up to heaven. That night I stood at my bedroom window, hoping to see the silvery soul of the pope rising from the earth.

The next afternoon, Jimmy and I took a hike in the woods. We reached an old stone wall, scrambled over it, and made a right turn. Sunlight filtered through the trees and danced along the path.

"This way," Jimmy said, pointing. I followed him. The air turned warm and heavy. And the ground felt spongy, like we were near a swamp. I smelled the sour odor of skunk cabbage. But Jimmy kept going, pushing through thick brush. It seemed like we were in the deepest, wildest part of the forest. All of a sudden, we stepped onto grass! Somebody's backyard! We saw two old people staring at us, a man and a woman. The man waved us over.

"C'mere!" he called. We walked carefully over the lawn to the brick patio. There was a neat row of rose bushes and a table set with a bowl of red grapes, a plate of sliced cheese, fancy crackers, and a bottle of wine.

"Hello there!" The woman spoke in a kindly voice. "I'm Sophie Pratt, and this is Arthur Pratt. Are you from around here?"

"Kind of," I said. We couldn't have been far from our house, but the smooth lawn and rose bushes made it seem like a whole different neighborhood.

"What are your names?"

"I'm Ralph."

"Jimmy."

"What's your last name?"

"Fletcher."

"The Fletchers!" Sophie Pratt gave us a huge grin. "We don't live but six houses away!"

My eyes wandered over to the grill. A whiff of burning charcoal grazed past my nose, carrying with it a sweet smell. My stomach growled. Mr. Pratt lifted the hood of the grill. Leaning forward, I saw two rows of clams cooking a few inches above the charcoal. I also saw what smelled so good: a little crock of melted butter.

"Best way to cook 'em," the man explained. "Heat makes 'em open right up. Want to try one?"

Jimmy shook his head. But I figured, why not? We weren't supposed to accept food from strangers, but these old people were neighbors. Mr. Pratt took one of the clams off the grill, lifted it from its shell, dunked it into that pot of melted butter, and popped it into my mouth.

"How was that, dear?" Sophie Pratt asked.

"Great," I said, nodding. It was so delicious I ate two more. Seeing my reaction, Jimmy ate a couple clams, too.

We left a little while later, promising to come back and visit soon. But I didn't see them until a month later. It was just another morning until Lainie came running in from outside.

"C'mon!" she yelled. "Emergency!"

"What?" I started pulling on sneakers.

"Some kind of bomb fell in the Pratts' front yard!"

"A bomb?!"

We sprinted down to the Pratts' house. There were police cars and lots of strange men I'd never seen before. Some were yelling, *"Stand back! Stand back!"* I saw an ugly hole maybe five feet long and three feet wide in the middle of the Pratts' front lawn. Water was gushing out, making pools on the grass, spilling onto the sidewalk, and streaming down one side of Acorn Street. I spotted Sophie Pratt standing near the hole. She was crying, with her husband beside her. Two policemen were talking to them. I saw Mr. Fishman, the father of my friend Steve.

"What happened?" I asked him. "Was it a bomb?"

"I don't think so." He shook his head. "A bomb

would've ripped a much bigger hole than that. Somebody said it was part of an airplane that fell off. Somebody else said it might be a dummy bomb."

"A dummy bomb?" I'd never heard of such a thing.

He shrugged. "Could be some kind of military gadget, maybe a test that went wrong. There are lots of rumors, but nobody seems to know."

More people kept arriving: women holding little babies, kids on bikes, a man taking pictures, men from the Marshfield Water Department. The water sluicing down Acorn Street turned everything muddy. Then some men showed up with fancy uniforms and unsmiling eyes. Soldiers. They set up a barricade and sealed off the street. This forced all the cars to turn around, even people who lived on Acorn Street. I wanted to stay and watch all the action but the soldiers made us go home.

The whole thing was pretty exciting, and it made me realize that there was a whole world out there—immense and dangerous—beyond the cozy world I knew on Acorn Street. We never did find out what happened, though one night I dreamed that it was the pope who fell out of heaven and punched a hole in the Pratts' lawn.

Lainie, Bobby, Jimmy, Tommy, and me.
Lainie and Jimmy are sick.

Teeth

MOM HAD A "tooth bank" shaped like a coconut. When one of our teeth came out, she washed off the blood and deposited the tooth into that bank.

"Why are you saving our teeth?" Jimmy wanted to know.

"Because." She smiled at him. "They're precious to me. And so are you."

Great Grandma came to visit two or three

times a year. She was old and tiny. Great Grandma always wore a gray sweatshirt way too big for her and smelled like the gingersnap cookies she baked. She put whole chunks of ginger into the cookies, so when I bit into them, they made my eyes water. I loved her with all my heart and pretended to love those cookies so I wouldn't hurt her feelings.

Great Grandma had a slow walk, and I liked to secretly follow her as she moved through the house or out in the yard. Her hearing wasn't very good so she never knew when I was spying on her.

Early one morning I heard her outside my bedroom, going downstairs. I waited until she reached the bottom stair before I got out of bed and followed her. She padded into the kitchen, dressed in slippers and the gray sweatshirt. What was she doing? Getting a snack? Making coffee? Moving closer, careful to stay out of sight, I saw her go into the pantry. I was amazed when she came out holding the tooth bank! She unscrewed the rubber plug on the bottom, emptied some teeth into her hand, and went out the back door.

I knew if I followed too closely she'd catch me spying, so I eased out the front door and ran around the house. The grass was a cold, wet shock to my bare feet. Stealing from tree to tree, I saw Great Grandma go into the garage. A minute later she came out carrying a trowel, then went to the vegetable garden in back of the house.

I crept up until I was about thirty feet away, close enough to see her kneel down and start digging a hole in the ground. She put one of the teeth into the hole, covered it with dirt, and patted it down. She did the same thing three more times. Then she turned around and moved slowly back toward the house.

I made myself wait five minutes, then five more, before going to the garden spot where she planted our teeth. I don't know what I expected to see. Finally, I went inside and snuck up to my bedroom.

I never told anyone about this, and Great Grandma never said anything, but I had a million questions in my head. Did she plant the teeth figuring they'd bring good luck to our house? Did she think they'd fertilize the tomatoes? Was she just plain crazy?

Nothing unusual sprouted in the garden that summer. But every time I went past that spot, I'd check to see if one of those teeth had taken root in the soil and started to grow.

Bobby, Tommy, Lainie, Jimmy, and me.

Words

STICKS AND STONES can break my bones, but words can never hurt me. That's what everyone said, but was it true? Words were tricky. They seemed to have a secret life of their own. Mom wrote the word *hear* and showed me the word *ear* that was hidden within it. That was cool. Sometimes a word had its own disguise, with a sound that didn't tell you which one it was. You could hear the word *see* but it might really be *sea*, or even the letter *C*. The same with *bare* and *bear*, *red* and *read*.

I was fascinated by swears too. Curse words. You could have a perfectly respectable word like *ship*, but change one letter at the end and you might get your mouth washed out with soap.

One day, Freddy Black, a kid who lived down the street, came to my house and taught me the worst swear you could possibly say. He said it to me just as my father came out of the garage, grunting under the weight of the storm windows he was carrying on his back. Dad hadn't heard, but the swear hung in the air, like a bad smell. I felt guilty, learning a nasty word like that while my father was working so hard.

"Can I help?" I asked Dad later that afternoon. He was outside the garage, dusting off the screen windows.

"Sure thing," he said, handing me a whisk broom. The day had grown cold and windy. The dirt I brushed off got blown back into my face.

"Hey, Dad," I asked, "if you say *Jesus*, is that a swear?"

"Depends on how you say it," he replied. "If you just say the name *Jesus*, it's okay. But if you take the Lord's name in vain, that's a swear, and it's wrong."

The trees sighed in the breeze. I had always wondered exactly what that meant: "take the Lord's name in vain." The wind blew again, a gust strong enough to twist the screen out of my hands.

"Jesus!" I yelled.

With that, Dad grabbed my arm, angrily swatted my bottom, and sent me into the house. My bottom hurt, but my feelings hurt even worse. Maybe words couldn't hurt you, but they sure could get you into trouble.

Mom holding Jimmy at Christmas.

Jimmy

WHEN JIMMY and I were in our bunk beds, we talked about everything. Most of the time I knew what he was thinking, and he knew my thoughts too.

One time, Jimmy led a bunch of kids through a part of Ale's Woods we'd never explored before. It was hot, and the rest of us wore shorts, but Jimmy always wore heavy jeans because he liked to climb through thickets of briars and prickers. His face was sweaty and streaked with dirt. We'd just entered a sunny meadow, running full speed, when Jimmy suddenly slammed on the brakes. He pointed at a wooden shack caved in on one side.

"C'mon!" he yelled.

Jimmy climbed in. I heard a muffled cry, and then he climbed out again. Everyone gasped: He was triumphantly holding two fistfuls of snakes! There must have been six of them in each hand, garter snakes twisting in the sunlight, furious that their sleeping place had been disturbed.

Another time, after a bad windstorm, Jimmy and I went hiking through a swampy part of the woods. The storm had knocked over a tree, and a shallow pool had formed in the crater left by the mass of uplifted roots. We went for a closer look, and as I moved to the water's edge, something lurched into the water.

"Did you see that?" Jimmy asked.

"Yeah." I nodded. "Looked like some kind of newt or salamander."

"That was no ordinary salamander," Jimmy informed me. "Didn't you see the red on its gills?"

At home Jimmy searched through the *World Book Encyclopedia* to find the animal he'd seen. For a long time he sat on the living room floor paging through volumes A (amphibians), L (lizards), and R (reptiles).

"Found it," he said, showing me the page. "A mud puppy. That's it. We saw a mud puppy."

Mud puppy! I fell in love with the odd name, the funny picture it made in my head. The name clicked. Pretty soon all the neighborhood kids were calling that uprooted tree Mud Puppy Place, although we never did see any mud puppies after that day in the woods.

Jimmy with a turtle he found in the woods.

School
Age 7

IT WAS TIME for me to start first grade. Jimmy stood with me at the bus stop. Mom waited with us.

"What are you going to do in school?" Jimmy asked, frowning.

"I don't know," I said. "Learn stuff."

"Why can't I come too?"

"You're not old enough," I told him.

"Next year," Mom said.

Jimmy kicked a stone across the street. Finally, the bus rumbled up, huge and yellow. It opened its doors; Jimmy stepped back as I climbed the stairs. I found a seat next to my friend Steve Fishman and waved through the window. Mom waved and flashed a big smile, but my brother kept both hands at his sides.

I liked school. And on that first day I knew I'd be good at it. I could just tell. I was good at figuring out what the teacher wanted me to do and exactly how she wanted me to do it—add, read, copy letters (though my handwriting was terrible). I even liked the hot dog, wax beans, and fried potatoes they served for lunch. The day flew by. That afternoon when I got off the bus, Jimmy was at the bus stop, tapping his feet, eagerly waiting for me.

"Look!" He had a small animal skull in his hands.

"What is it?"

"I think it's a beaver," he said. "Too big to be a cat. I found the bones in the woods. Here. It's for you."

The next day when I stepped off the bus he

gave me an old wasp nest. Every day, as soon as I got off the bus, he'd hand me a treasure he'd found in the woods.

I knew Jimmy would be going to school soon, and I was worried about him. I tried to get him ready for it.

"It's not like home," I said. "You've got to follow the rules, or you'll get in trouble."

"What rules?"

"Like, you can't just talk whenever you want," I explained. "You raise your hand if you want to say something. Okay?"

"Okay!" Eyes closed, he raised his hand and pointed straight up.

"This is serious," I told him. "Do you know the Pledge of Allegiance?"

"The what?" he asked. I made him stand with me in the kitchen, put his hand on his heart, and pledge allegiance to an imaginary flag on the wall. Jimmy groaned and rolled his eyes.

"They say the Pledge every morning, so you've got to know it, and you've got to know it by heart," I said, jabbing him lightly in the chest. "Better learn it now."

The following September, the big day came. Jimmy held my hand and giggled nervously when the bus arrived. We ran up the stairs together, and Jimmy sat on the edge of his seat all the way to school. When we got there, a woman met us and pinned a paper circle to his shirt. My brother shot me one last look before the lady led him away.

That day I spotted Jimmy only once, walking in a line with other kids, headed into the cafeteria. In the woods he always knew exactly where he was. But standing in that noisy cafeteria, with his freckles and thick glasses and cowlicky hair, Jimmy looked lost.

When Jimmy got off the bus that afternoon he went straight to the woods. I didn't see him again until supper time.

That night I asked Jimmy if he liked school.

"Boring." He didn't want to talk about it.

And that's the way it was for him every day. He'd come home and go straight to the woods. He didn't even wait to change out of his school clothes or eat a snack.

School was fine for a kid like me, because I knew how to shut up and listen. But it seemed wrong to take an outside kid like Jimmy and lock him inside for six hours a day. They should have had a different kind of school for Jimmy, maybe a place with acres of unexplored woods and streams and swamps and steep rocky cliffs where he could spend hours making forts or digging for fossils and animal bones.

In November we got report cards. I sneaked a peek at Jimmy's. His grades were lower than mine, a lot lower, which didn't make any sense. I knew that Jimmy was smarter than me, but on that report card, there was no grade for knowing where snakes sleep in the heat of day, for being able to tell the difference between the skull of a cat or a beaver, a salamander or a mud puppy. It wasn't fair, but I told myself that the woods would always be the place where Jimmy learned best. In that school he would always be a straight-A student.

Little Ralph and big Ralph.

First Pen
Age 8

WHEN I WAS EIGHT, Dad bought me a pen. It was just a cheap BIC, the kind with a clear barrel so you could see how much ink was left in the cartridge. Still, I loved it. In school we wrote in pencil, so putting inked words onto a piece of paper really made me feel grown-up.

With that pen and a brand-new notebook I made my first story. I wrote it on a rainy Sunday, sitting at the kitchen table while Mom made caramel apples with the little kids. The story was about a major-league baseball player who batted 1.000 during his rookie year. The player was amazing—he got a hit every time he came to bat. No pitcher could figure out how to strike him out!

It was fun writing that story. And it felt like a small miracle, too: First there was nothing on the page, then the story appeared, written in ink that couldn't be erased.

I sat for a long time, wondering what to write next. I stared at my BIC, the cartridge filled with blue so dark it was almost black. What words were hidden—unborn, unwritten—in all that unused ink?

Goofing around with my brothers and sister.

Scuttlebutt

IN CLASS WE GOT seated alphabetically by our last names. Karen Aaronburg always sat in the first seat, front row. Not only did Karen's last name begin with an *A*, but the letter that followed was another *A*. So Karen Aaronburg had a lock on that first seat, and she sat on it like no one on earth could ever take it away.

Since my last name began with an *F*, I often got

seated in the first seat, second row, right next to Karen Aaronburg. That suited me fine. Maybe she was a little snotty, but I liked her face, especially those bright blue eyes.

One morning we were having snack. I had just started to eat a carrot when I felt her eyes on me.

"Have you heard the scuttlebutt?" she asked.

"Huh?" I wasn't sure I heard her right.

"The scuttlebutt," she repeated. "Do you know what that word means?"

"Yeah!" I lied.

"It means gossip," she explained.

"Hey, I know, I know."

"Well, have you heard the scuttlebutt?" she asked again.

"No." I tried to look disinterested.

"Well, do you want to hear?" She gave me a straight look. "It's about you, sort of."

"What?"

Leaning forward, she motioned me closer.

"Your mother is going to have another baby."

I stared at her, unable to tell if she was mocking me or acting smug or enjoying the shocked look that must have been plastered all over my face. She simply stared back, and her face had never looked quite so wide awake as it did at that moment.

"No way," I finally said.

"It's true," she replied, nodding. "Ask your mother."

I had to sit through four more hours before I could check the truth of this story. When I got off the bus, I rushed into the house and kitchen.

"A girl in school told me you were going to have another baby," I sputtered. "Is that true?"

Mom looked at me with raised eyebrows.

"Well . . . yes," she admitted with a shy smile. "Isn't that wonderful?"

"But why didn't *you* tell me?"

"Dad and I weren't quite ready," she said. "We were going to tell you in a few weeks. Who was the girl?"

"Karen Aaronburg."

"Oh." Mom nodded. "I think I know what

happened. I mentioned it to Polly Renshaw. Polly and Beth Aaronburg are first cousins. Polly must've told Beth, and Beth told Karen."

"And Karen told me," I said. "Mom! It would be nice if I knew before every other kid in school!"

"You're right," Mom agreed. "I'm sorry."

By Christmas vacation, Mom was going around saying, "I'm a house, aren't I?" Nobody disagreed. She looked like she was about to burst. In late January we all came home from school to find a new baby boy, Johnny, in the bassinet.

Next school year, right after Thanksgiving, Karen motioned me close to her.

"I've got more scuttlebutt," she said softly.

"What?" My cheeks burned like she'd just smacked me, hard. "A baby?"

"Yeah, another one." Karen gave me a knowing smile. "Mom told me last night. Hey, I'm trying to figure out all the kids in your family. Is this right? Seven kids? Am I missing anybody?"

She handed me a piece of paper with this list written on it:

Ralph
Jimmy
Lainie
Tommy
Bobby
Johnny
new baby

I turned away without answering. Her list was accurate, but I was so mad I couldn't even look at her. And Karen seemed to understand, because she didn't say another word about it for the rest of the day.

"Are you pregnant again, Mom?" I blurted out that afternoon.

At first she looked confused.

"Yes, oh goodness, I'm sorry!" She apologized for not telling me, but what good did that do? That night, at supper, Mom shared the news with the whole family.

"Lainie, this time when I go to the hospital, maybe I'll bring you back a little sister!"

Lainie smiled at that. But four months later, on the first day of spring, we all came home to find baby number seven, Joey, asleep in the bassinet.

Johnny and Joey in front, with Jimmy, me, Tommy, and Lainie in back.

Farmed Out

WHEN MOM got pregnant her belly swelled like bread dough rising. And when it came time to deliver the baby everybody got sent to stay with relatives. Lainie went to Grandma and Aunt Mary's house in Arlington. Tommy and Bobby went to Grandma and Grandpa's house in Fall River. Jimmy and I got the best deal of all: We went to Uncle Paul and Aunt Louise's house in Rhode Island. And they had as many kids as we did.

Aunt Louise was French Canadian. Uncle Paul was Dad's oldest brother. He was an English professor. He'd sit around the house reading thick books and smoking a pipe, calmly ignoring the deafening racket made by all the kids running and yelling around him.

Getting farmed out was terrific. Aunt Louise never made us clean dishes off the table or do any chores. We didn't even have to make our beds. For breakfast she cooked fried-eggs-on-toast sandwiches—they were so delicious I couldn't stop eating them. On warm days we always went to the beach. In the late afternoon we'd walk to Brooms, a store that sold nothing but penny candy. When it got dark we ran through the neighborhood playing Flashlight Tag and Hide-and-Seek until the lawns turned cool and moist and bats began to appear in the sky.

Aunt Louise dialed our number so Jimmy and I could talk to Mom and Dad. "So you don't get homesick," she said. But honestly, I didn't really miss them. I felt a little guilty about that, but it was true. It seemed like I had shed my tight family skin for something bigger, looser, more comfortable, if only for a few days.

Me, age three, feeding a bottle to Lainie, while Jimmy feeds himself.

Baby

"CAN WE GET a pet?" Lainie asked. "A kitten? A dog? Please?"

Every year we posed the question. We begged, we pleaded, but Mom and Dad always had the same answer.

"We've already got enough little animals running around here," they said. "God knows we don't need another."

In our house, most of the action took place in

55

the kitchen: Mom talking on the telephone, kids and friends eating popcorn or slurping watermelon or sucking Popsicles and jabbering nonstop around the big table. The kitchen was the heart of our house, and the baby's playpen stood in the center of the kitchen.

I never got used to the calm, knowing look in Karen Aaronburg's eyes when she turned to ask "Have you heard the scuttlebutt?" But I sure had gotten used to babies, because Mom brought them home from the hospital, regular as a once-a-year holiday.

The newest baby stayed close to Mom for the first few months, nursing, sleeping a lot. We had a creaky white bassinet with wooden wheels so you could move it around the house. When the baby reached six months, it graduated into the playpen. And this meant that whoever had been in the playpen got released from the baby cage—free!—so it could stagger unsteadily around the house, pulling everything it could reach off shelves and tables, leaving a mess wherever it went.

I loved the Fletcher baby, whoever it was, whatever its name. I loved the pudgy little body, the gummy grins, the milky breath, the soft spot on top of its head. I loved coming in from outside to see my big-eyed little creature in the playpen, drooling, yelling, cooing, laughing, fussing, peek-a-booing, its head swiveling this way and that trying to follow all the antics of the big kids.

Mom barely had a second to breathe, what with doing laundry, answering the phone, cooking supper, or nursing the new baby. So when the baby started crying, I helped out. We all did. I knew how to pick up the baby and tell if its diaper was dirty or clean by how spongy it was. I knew how to change dirty diapers (and avoid the messiest ones), how to pin the cloth diapers without poking the baby. I was good at telling the difference between *I'm-really-hungry* crying and *I'm-just-bored* fussing. I loved the taste of baby food (and always sneaked a few bites when Mom wasn't looking). I knew how to warm up a bottle of milk in a saucepan on the stove and squirt a little on my wrist to make sure the milk wasn't too hot. I could pick up the baby and walk around with it, cocking my right hip, so the baby would have a nice little ledge to sit on while I held it snug with one hand and rummaged through the cabinet for a teething biscuit with the other.

With the eternal Fletcher baby sitting in the playpen, year after year, I sort of became an expert on the subject.

Bobby.

Bobby

BOBBY WAS BABY number five. He sat in the playpen happy as pie, like he had no idea what was coming, which of course he didn't. How could he? How could any of us? Bobby seemed no different from the rest of us—he ate, slept, played, argued, laughed, watched TV, took baths, rode the school bus, complained about having to go to church. But he wasn't like the rest of us. Bobby never got the chance to grow up. In his last year of high school he was killed in a car accident.

When he was little I remember walking into the kitchen and seeing his head through the slats in the playpen. The front of his shirt was soaked with drool. Mom said he was cutting his first tooth, but he seemed content, talking to himself as he turned the crank on his jack-in-the-box. I tried to sneak past, but Bobby saw me and made a loud sound, extending his little arms straight up into the air like, touchdown! Which meant, pick me up! I'm a sucker for that move. No possible way I could ignore it.

"Okay, hold your horses, hold your horses," I told him. Bending down, I grabbed him firmly under both armpits, and he made a happy gur-gling sound, like a baby's idea of a song, as I lifted his soft little body into my arms. He was a real good baby and a terrific brother. Not a day goes by that I don't miss him.

Bobby and Johnny
at the edge of our woods.

Daily Life
Age 9

WE DIDN'T LIVE in a very big house. Mom and Dad had a bedroom downstairs. Lainie and the baby slept upstairs in a tiny bedroom. The other upstairs bedroom was a big, half-finished room with three sets of bunk beds. All the boys slept there. The bedroom was always a lively place with lots of hysterical laughter as two brothers made a sneak attack on one bunk bed or another two counterattacked with a barrage of stuffed animals, thrown from one side of the room to the other.

The bathroom was far away, so Mom put an empty milk bottle in the middle of the room. At night, if any of us boys had to pee, instead of walking all the way to the bathroom we peed into the bottle. That milk bottle was convenient, but it created a monumental mess if someone accidentally knocked it over, which happened more than once.

My brothers and I loved to jump up and touch the wood above the doorways. Every few weeks Mom had to climb up on a chair to clean off our fingerprints.

When Mom went food shopping, she always filled two carts to the very top. We helped her lug the bags of food into the house, and then she started cooking dinner. One night she served everybody but by the time she finally sat down to eat, all of us had finished and were ready for dessert. Mom did not look amused.

"This is not going to work," she hissed slowly. The next night at supper, we started a new routine. All the kids had to wait, folding our hands, until she finally had the chance to sit down. After Dad said grace, we were allowed to start eating.

"Ten minutes," Mom reminded us when the meal ended, and we knew what that meant. Everyone pitched in to clean up from supper. With so many hands working together, we could always make the kitchen look spotless in ten minutes or less.

With such a big family, Mom and Dad created lots of rituals like that to keep the family running smoothly. But some of our rituals were a little odd, like when Mom motioned us into the living room and told us to "snick up" the rug.

"Aw, Mom," Jimmy moaned. "I want to go outside."

"C'mon," she said. "It won't take five minutes."

At that word—*snick*—each of us got down on all fours and started picking up tiny bits of dirt, dust, and lint from the rug. I grabbed a piece of dirt, tucked it neatly into my palm, and scooted forward to pick up some more. Everyone helped;

even the baby pitched in. With so many kids, plus Mom, it didn't take long before the rug looked nice and clean again.

The same ritual took place every night, and I never gave it a second thought. It's not as if we were poor. We had a TV and a car. We had a vacuum cleaner too, but for some reason we never used it at the end of the day. Instead, we snicked. And I figured that the same thing must be happening in every other house in town—mothers and kids getting down on their hands and knees to snick up the rug before Dad got home from work.

Me, Jimmy, Bobby, and Joey
with stamps Aunt Mary gave us.

A Pox upon Us All

WE KIDS DID everything together. We sat at the same table, eating the same food, breathing the same air. We shared jokes, songs, glasses, towels, and toys. We loved to set up a line of blocks so that when you toppled one it would start a chain reaction and knock them down all the way from the living room to the bathroom.

We shared the same germs too. First one of us

would catch a cold or cough or flu, then another kid would get it a day or so later, followed by another and another . . . until there were so many sick kids lying around the house, it felt like we were living in a hospital.

When I was really sick I got to sleep downstairs in Mom and Dad's bed during the day. I loved that. The saddest part for me was when other kids got sick and I got evicted from the big bed. Usually Mom forbade us to turn on the TV during the day, but when we were sick she made an exception and let us watch for an hour or so.

I loved being sick, because that's when I got extra-special care from Mom. She would fix me soup or an egg on toast for lunch. When my nose got plugged up or I had a bad cough, she rubbed Vicks on my chest. But I never got a really big slice of Mom's time because there were always babies and toddlers at home, and she had her hands full with them.

The winter I was nine we all got chicken pox at the same time. Mom about wore herself out trying to take care of us. It got so bad that Dad stayed home from work to help out.

"Don't scratch!" Mom kept saying as we picked at the sores on our bodies. She gave us baths with baking soda, which left a strange, gritty residue at the bottom of the tub. For the first few days we were perfectly content lying around the house in our pajamas, doing puzzles, reading comics, watching daytime TV. But being cooped up inside soon made us restless. We needed an outlet for all that pent-up energy.

Mom took the baby to the store to buy some food. The instant she drove away, we started racing through the house, yelling at the top of our lungs, having wild pillow fights, completely forgetting that we were sick. When Mom came home she scolded us for messing up the house. The next day our muscles hurt, and Mom said we had used them too quickly after being sick for so long.

The chicken pox lasted more than a week. Eventually, we were healthy enough to go back to school. But two weeks later we were all sick again.

The six of us could do nothing more than lay in our beds, limp as rag dolls. I had a headache and an earache, plus it felt like there was an achy fire in the joints of my shoulders, arms, and legs.

The doorbell rang. I felt too weak to go answer it. A man's voice boomed through the front door. A moment later Mom led Dr. Wentworth into the living room. He was a friendly, handsome doctor who came to our house four or five times a year.

"They're *all* sick?" he asked. "How about the baby?"

"No," Mom said. "At least, not yet."

"Well, well, well," Dr. Wentworth said. "Let's see what we're dealing with."

Mom called us all into the living room. Dr. Wentworth sat us in one long row on the couch. Then he went to work, poking backs and bellies and necks, peering into our mouths and ears, listening with his stethoscope to seven beating hearts.

"Does it hurt to swallow?"

Nod.

"Do you feel tired?"

Nod.

"They've got swollen glands, every one of them, and that tells me one thing," he told my mother. "They've got the mumps. There's a lot of it going around."

"Mumps!" Mom cried. "How long will it last?"

"Figure a good week," the doctor said.

"A good week?" Mom just stared at him.

"Keep doing what you're doing," Dr. Wentworth told her. "Give them lots of liquids and lots of rest. Kids are pretty resilient. They'll survive."

"I know they'll survive," Mom said, sighing and picking up the baby who had started to cry. "It's me I'm not so sure about."

The five oldest kids in summer.

Eating the World

JIMMY DIDN'T LIKE following the rules, but Tommy took the rules and shredded them into little pieces. From the moment he could walk, he was the Tasmanian devil of the family, pulling books off shelves, whacking the little kids, stealing toys.

One time he yelled during church.

"Quiet!" Mom told him. "The priest doesn't want to hear you."

"I hate the priest," Tommy said loudly. With that, Mom grabbed his arm and rushed him out of church.

Whenever he got into trouble, Mom made him sit under the kitchen table so she could keep an eye on him. This happened a lot.

One morning Tommy wandered away from our house and walked down Acorn Street. He was four years old and, somehow, got the crazy-fool idea to start eating things. He munched dande-lions. He gobbled grass, chewed sticks, swallowed dirt. Tommy pried some used gum off the street and chewed it. He found a discarded cigarette, broke it in half, and gobbled that down too.

Pretty soon Tommy staggered into the house, his face white as a piece of Wonder Bread. He was crying and holding his belly. When Mom found out what he'd been eating she let out a yelp. She asked Lainie to watch the baby and keep an eye on the other kids. Then she put Tommy into the back seat of the car and drove straight to the hospital. I went with her.

"What's going to happen to him?" I asked.

"He might have to get his stomach pumped," Mom said. I could tell she was upset; she had the steering wheel in a stranglehold.

"Really? How do they do that?" I pictured some kind of suction on the outside of his belly.

"They take a skinny hose and stick it down your throat," Mom explained, using a low voice so Tommy couldn't overhear. "They vacuum up whatever's in your stomach. Believe me, it's not a pleasant experience."

"Ugh!" I wanted to throw up just listening to the description.

It turned out that Tommy didn't have to get his stomach pumped after all. The doctor gave him a special kind of medicine that made him vomit all the junk he'd eaten. I stayed in the waiting room, so I missed those fireworks. When Mom finally brought my brother out he looked a lot better, even though he was crying.

"You're lucky you didn't kill yourself," Mom said on the way home. I turned to look at Tommy, but he had already fallen asleep.

✦ ✦ ✦

Next day at breakfast, Jimmy asked him, "Why'd you do something dumb like that?"

"I was hungry," Tommy replied.

"Why didn't you eat some regular food?" Jimmy demanded.

"I didn't have any," Tommy explained.

"That's the stupidest excuse I've ever heard," Jimmy said, rolling his eyes.

What Tommy did *was* stupid, but for a long time the idea of it—trying to eat the world— stayed in my mind. Once, when I was alone in the woods, I pulled a leaf off a maple tree, folded it into my mouth, and started to chew. It was bitter. Later I nibbled on a piece of pine bark and spit it out. I knelt down, peeled off the layer of pine needles, and put my tongue against the bare ground. Dirt tasted different from what I expected. It was almost clean, almost sweet.

Tommy, Lainie, me, and Bobby.

Summer Sunday Morning

Saturday morning I went to confession, and at night I took a bath. Mom filled the tub, and we filed in like the animals on Noah's ark, two at a time, so she could scrub us clean. All this was because of Sunday. Sunday meant clean ears and wool pants, white shirts and ties, jackets and dresses, and shiny shoes. Sunday meant church.

I knew that going to confession and church was

a way to cleanse my soul, and it was important to have a clean, sin-free soul if you hoped to go to heaven. But church was important for another, more practical reason. If we behaved at church, if one of us didn't poke out somebody's eye while we were driving home, Dad would stop at Leo's Bakery for a dozen doughnuts. And Leo's lemon-filled doughnuts were so delicious that people traveled from far away to buy them.

But going to church in Marshfield got a lot more complicated in the summer. Tourists swelled our town from Memorial Day straight through to Labor Day. Streets, stores, and churches were a lot more crowded. One morning we showed up for the 9:30 mass to find our church packed, every seat taken.

Jimmy groaned. I looked at Dad and Mom. What were we going to do? Go home and come back for the eleven o'clock mass early enough to get a proper seat? Not likely. What would we do at home for an hour and a half sitting around in our best clothes? How could we possibly keep them clean?

I knew the bottom line: If you were there on time, it "counted" for your Sunday mass obligation, even if you didn't actually get a seat in the church. There was no choice but to wait with other latecomers by the open door outside the church.

So we stood, all nine of us, outside the big church door. Dad slipped through the crowd and ducked inside. I knew he would whisper a few quiet words with the ushers and leave a small stack of quarters on one of the felt-covered tables at the back of the church. I wished I could go in with him. It was hard to hear what the priest was saying. In fact, it was impossible to hear more than the sound of droning words, the occasional tinkle of bells on the altar, the rustle of people's best clothes as two hundred people all stood, sat, or knelt.

With no pews to corral them and no altar to focus their attention, my brothers and sisters showed no interest in what was going on inside. Outside the church they had no fear of God. Jimmy and Elaine began a contest to see how long they could balance on one foot. Tommy was hard at work bothering some ants. Bobby and Johnny were ripping pretend farts by blowing into their hands, much to the delight of Joey, the baby.

"Lemon doughnuts!" I reminded my brothers and sisters, but they ignored me.

When Mom saw what the kids were doing, she fiercely snapped her finger and fired a stern look at them. She grabbed Tommy and Bobby and pulled them close to the church door. For the next forty-five minutes she kept doing that, rotating kids close to the open door of the church so we could each get our dose of the churchy sounds, smells, and action.

Honestly, it seemed pretty pointless to me, standing there in our best clothes. I mean, the priest couldn't even see us! But when it became clear that we weren't going to leave, I realized that there was nothing to do but lean toward the open door, try to listen, and breathe in the incense smell wafting out into the June morning.

It was a perfect Marshfield morning, sunny and

warm. The air had a salty tang that tasted like the ocean. At this time of day it would be so beautiful at the beach. My wool pants were starting to itch, but I thought about Leo's Bakery and tried to hang in there. I had Jesus on the inside, sweet summer outside, and the possibility of some heavenly doughnuts not too far down the road.

My father.

Last Kiss

Mom and dad always kissed us good night before we went to bed. Mom kissed my right cheek, Dad my left. After that, I got under the covers and it was an easy glide to sleep.

These kisses were a regular part of the bedtime routine, like brushing my teeth, having the nightly bowl of cereal, or hearing a story before lights-out. It felt like having air to breathe or a blanket to keep me warm—*automatic*—and I never gave it a second thought.

One night I finished my bedtime bowl of cereal and went to Mom.

"Sleep tight," she murmured, kissing me on the cheek.

"Night, Mom."

I found Dad sitting at the desk in his office.

"I'm going to bed," I told him.

"Well, good night." To my great surprise, he reached out and shook my hand. At first I just stood there, confused. Finally I took his hand and shook it the way I'd seen men shake hands.

"Sleep tight," he said. Then he turned away from me and went back to his paperwork.

Feeling more surprised than hurt, I headed off to bed. Next night I gave it another shot. After eating my bowl of cereal I went to Mom. She kissed me and gave me a big hug. That built up my courage before I went to my dad. I found him out on the driveway. He was packing the trunk of his car, getting ready to go on a business trip.

"Hey," he said, straightening up. "Bedtime?"

"Yeah." I moved toward him.

"Good night." He wrapped his arms around me and gave me a bear hug.

"Night." My voice was muffled against his chest. He released me and went back to packing the car. For a few seconds I didn't move. The night was warm. Fireflies were out, floating on the evening breeze. They made me think of the jellyfish Dad and I saw one night about a year before when we were on a dock at the beach. I noticed lights flickering in the dark water, and was amazed to find out that they were living animals.

"How can they light up like that?" I had asked my dad.

"They make their own light," he explained. "Like fireflies."

"How do jellyfish move?" I asked him. "Do they have fins?"

"No," Dad said.

"But what if they want to see their friends?" I asked. "How do they get there?"

"They drift in the tide," Dad explained. "If they're lucky, the tide will help them drift to where they want to go."

"What if they want to see their friends but they're not lucky?" I asked.

He shrugged.

"Then I guess they drift away from each other."

Two more times I went to Dad for a good-night kiss. No luck. Finally I gave up. Mom still kissed me good night on my right cheek, but somehow it didn't feel the same. Her kisses didn't have the safe, solid feeling they'd had before.

I laid in bed trying to figure it out. Even though I was confused, one thing seemed clear—my father and I had drifted away from each other in a small but important way, a way that I couldn't explain, not even to myself.

Joey, me, Andy Hunt,
Steve Fishman, and Jimmy.

Friends
Age 10

ANDY HUNT LIVED next door. I loved the way his eyes crinkled up when he heard something funny. When Andy laughed, the whole world lit up, like the sun coming from behind a cloud. His black hair hung straight down, and he'd shake water out of it, like a wet dog, after we went swimming. Every day I knocked on his back door or he knocked on mine. If he wasn't home I'd wait for him outside, and it seemed like forever until the Hunts' car finally pulled into the driveway and Andy ran over to play.

Steve Fishman lived on a small farm that was visible from our house, though you had to cross Route 3A to get to it, and that was a busy road. He was one of the only Jewish kids I knew. The kitchen in his house had a wild, spicy smell that I loved. Steve and I played music in his room, fooled around with his father's barbells, and talked endlessly about a girl we both loved.

Mr. Fishman was strict: Steve had an unbelievable number of chores to do before he could play with me. I helped him so he'd get done faster, but sometimes Steve ran off before his chores were finished. When that happened, his father always found out and sent Steve to his room. Mr. Fishman never told me I had to leave, but with Steve in his room, there was nothing for me to do, so I'd get on my bike and ride home. I took it hard whenever my friends got punished. It felt like I was getting punished too.

Larry Waters lived down the street in an old farmhouse that had all kinds of attics, tool sheds, root cellars, workshops, garages, hay lofts with real trapdoors, barns and even an under barn. It was the perfect house for playing Hide-and-Seek. Or War. I loved going over there. There were ten kids in Larry's family, and his house was always jammed with toys.

Larry had a Milky Way of freckles and a mane of red hair, and he was the strongest kid I knew. I guess he'd been toughened up from the pounding he got from his big brothers. But those brothers passed down some great-looking sweaters to him, and Larry ranked us out for the pitiful clothes we wore. He had style, and he could curse like nobody's business. When he opened his mouth a fantastic flood of swears would come spilling out. I don't mean one or two, I mean a whole stream of interconnected curses.

And Larry was funny too. One of the commercials on TV had a jingle that went like this:

"My advice, sir,
Get De-Icer . . ."

Larry preferred to sing the song this way:

"My advice, sir,
Treat my friends nicer
Or you'll get a big fat lip . . ."

The four of us—Andy, Larry, Steve, and I—
were all in the same grade. We called ourselves
the Four Stooges. With my brother Jimmy, I spent
most of the time in the woods, climbing trees,
exploring, looking for stuff. With my friends, I
spent more time inside talking and trying to crack
open the great mysteries—death, God, girls. One
day we talked about kissing.

"Thing is, you don't just kiss her quick and
then it's over," Larry said.

"Yeah," Andy agreed.

"What would you know?" Larry shot back.
"Your ma's the only girl you ever kissed!"

Laughter.

"Kissing takes a long time," Larry continued. "One kiss might last five, ten minutes."

Pause.

"Yeah," Steve put in. "You got to hold your breath."

"Tough luck, guys." Larry grinned, leaned back, and loudly cracked his knuckles. "I can hold my breath fifteen seconds longer than any of you jokers. So when it comes to kissing, I'll be king."

Bobby at Rexhame Beach.

Jonathan Miller

ANDY, STEVE, AND LARRY were my best friends. But in some ways my closest best friend was a boy named Jonathan Miller. I met him one summer day at Humarock Beach. We spent no more than five hours together, but I've never forgotten him.

I spotted him standing on one foot at the shore.

"I found some snew." I realized he was talking to me.

"What's snew?" I asked.

"I don't know," he replied, grinning. "What's new with you?"

I stared, not sure whether to laugh *with* him or *at* him.

"Look at that." He pointed at three little kids trying to dig a wall to protect a sand castle. The tide was coming in, fast, and the castle was in big trouble. He gave me a disgusted look. "They're doing it all wrong. You need to dig a ditch, a real big one."

"Yeah, like a moat," I agreed. "With a wall behind it."

We jumped in to help the little kids. I started making a big sand wall as the first line of defense while Jonathan raced around the beach gathering seaweed and pieces of driftwood to reinforce the wall. My brother Jimmy and two other kids came over to help, all of us digging like crazy. Waves kept attacking, and we kept fighting them off. We managed to protect the castle for another half hour until a big wave finally flattened it.

Jonathan was from Oregon and was visiting his

grandparents. Right away I loved him the way you love a best friend. I loved the funny faces he made while telling a stupid joke. We hung around together all day: swimming, looking for shells and sea glass and bottle caps. We built our own sand fort higher up the beach and ate lunch there. Two of my brothers wanted to come in the fort, but I shooed them away. I wasn't ready to share Jonathan, not yet.

I wished I'd brought something of mine to give him—the inside of a golf ball, an arrowhead, my shark-tooth fossil—but I'd come to the beach with nothing.

"We could be blood brothers," I said. "We'd need a knife, or a sharp shell. Then we have to cut our fingers so the blood can run together."

"We don't need to," Jonathan said, leaning back in the fort. "We're already blood brothers. I know we are."

"Yeah," I said because it was true.

At four o'clock his grandmother yelled. Time for him to go.

"Bye," he said.

"Bye." The lump in my throat made it hard to talk. He started walking away, turned back once to wave, then ran to catch up with his grandparents.

I never saw him again. But whenever anybody mentions Oregon, I always think of Jonathan.

Johnny and Joey meet Santa Claus.

The Sound in the Wall
Age 11

My FRIEND JIMMY DEAN invited me to his birthday party. I'd never been to his house before. Marshfield was a historic place with lots of old houses, and Jimmy Dean lived in one of the oldest houses in town, built in the early 1700s, according to Mom.

"Come in!" somebody yelled when I rang the doorbell. I stepped inside and walked down a short hallway into the kitchen. Two big girls stood there staring at me. They looked like high school kids.

"Where's Jimmy?" I asked.

"We're his sisters," one girl said. "What's your name?"

"Ralph."

"Don't worry, he'll be right down, Ralphie," the other girl replied. She looked at the present I'd brought. "Just stick that on the bench."

The girls stood beside a table with a big pile of raw hamburger meat on it. They were using their hands to form the red meat into flat patties and lining up the uncooked burgers on wax paper.

"I think he's kind of cute," the taller girl said. She stared at me and smiled. When I didn't smile back, the other one laughed.

"Don't look so serious!" She picked up a small ball of uncooked meat, sprinkled salt on it, and popped it into her mouth. I nearly gagged.

"It's good raw," she told me. "You ought to try some."

"Where's Jimmy?" I asked again.

"Don't worry, he's coming."

"Hey," one girl said, glancing slyly at her sister. "I'll show Ralphie the wall. C'mon, kiddo, this is something you don't want to miss." She rinsed off her hands and walked into a small room next to the kitchen. I hesitated for a few seconds before following her. The girl brought me over to the wall and pushed my head so my ear was flush against it. "Hear anything?"

I shook my head. She leaned against me, pressing my ear tighter to the wall. I smelled raw hamburger, but also the salty scent of her skin.

She whispered into my ear, "It helps if you close your eyes."

I tried that and suddenly I did hear it. A low sound, steady yet ragged, almost like a cat's purr, but wilder, more insistent.

"What is it?"

"Bees," she murmured. "A giant beehive. They've taken over the whole wall. You like honey, don't you, honey?" She was teasing me, but I didn't care. I was hypnotized by that sound, and the way it felt to have her pressing against me.

"You should get an exterminator," I said.

"But we don't want to," she hissed softly. "We like our bees."

I stood there, transfixed, unable to move, caught between her body and the sound of those bees. There must have been thousands of them, maybe millions. They sounded awfully hungry.

"Go on," she whispered. "Take a really good listen."

She leaned against me a little harder, and the buzzing grew louder. It seemed to spread from the wall into my ear, to the side of my face, down my neck. The feeling moved through me until it felt like the wall, the girl, and I were all buzzing together.

"Fletch!"

It was Jimmy Dean, staring at me. "What're you doing?"

"The bees . . ." I told him, pointing at the wall. Jimmy gave his big sister an annoyed look.

"C'mon, we're going to play War!" he yelled.

He raced out of the room with me following close behind. It felt good to be moving at full speed, past the grinning girls, past the pile of uncooked hamburger meat on the table, through the back screen door, until we burst together into the blinding sunlight like a couple of bees released from a jar.

Jimmy and me.

War

WE LOVED WAR. There were always enough kids around to play football or baseball or Hide-and-Seek or Kick-the-Can, and those games were fun. But good old War was the best game we played, by far, and we went at it every chance we got.

There were ten kids at Jimmy Dean's birthday party, and we quickly divided into two armies. Then there was a frantic scramble as we each tried to find the right gun. A short, gun-shaped stick made an excellent pistol. Longer sticks became rifles, and if there was a twig or bump at the end you had a telescopic sight. I made a machine gun out of a stick two feet long with a thicker piece at the base I could steady against my shoulder.

Weapons mattered. Plenty of times I started a battle holding nothing but a skinny twig or funny-shaped board. There was nothing better than having the right gun. I always felt dangerous when I was fully armed, packing serious heat.

War was simple: We hunted each other. All of us had seen enough movies and TV shows to know how to make war. We knew how to stay low, how to use trees and rocks for cover, how to crawl under bushes and clothes-ripping briars. When we got close enough to an exposed enemy soldier, we opened fire by sounding a single *pow!* or a *brrrrp!* burst of machine-gun fire.

"*Ba-da-da-da-da-da-da-da!*" I screamed at Jimmy Dean. "Got you!"

"You wish!" he yelled back from behind a bush.

"Hey, I *smoked* you! You're dead!"

"No way! I jumped back!"

"I killed you! You're gone!"

Nothing on earth was more thrilling than stealing close enough to get a clean shot at a real, live enemy soldier. To be good at War you had to know how to sneak, stalk, and shoot. But the most important thing was knowing how to die.

Each of us died differently. When Steve got hit he let out an *"ugh,"* grabbed his gut, and did a neat forward flip that sent him rolling over and over before he finally lay still. I admired that move a lot and tried to copy it. When someone shot Jimmy Dean, he dropped his gun and fell straight back. Andy often got shot, but most times he refused to die. Now he grabbed his right arm, face twisted in horrible pain.

"Arggh!" he screamed.

"What's wrong?" Larry yelled.

"I'm hit! Send reinforcements!" Andy screamed, his limb dangling uselessly. In the midst of a ferocious firefight, Larry rushed over, half-dragging, half-supporting Andy until Andy could scramble to safety.

Suddenly Jimmy jumped up and blasted Larry. Larry stopped and swayed for a second, hanging in the air, slack-jawed. Then he fell straight forward, allowing his face to mash into the dirt.

For years I had studied Larry's technique. I tried it myself at home when nobody was around, falling forward in a pile of leaves, letting my body drop like dead weight. But no matter how many times I practiced or how hard I tried, some stubborn part of me—arm, leg, or knee—insisted on reaching out at the last minute to break my fall. I finally gave up and accepted the truth. I'd never be able to die like Larry. None of us could.

I was moving along the side of the house when Steve Fishman jumped out in front of me. There was no place to hide. He fired at me point-blank, and I jerked back three times like I'd been punched in the chest. My eyes took on a dazed look, my body went limp, and I fell, spinning to one side and rolling over four times. Then I lay without moving a muscle, slowly counting to sixty. Finally I sat up, grinning, knowing I died well.

That moment reminded me of when I used to play Statue with Mom and Dad when I was little. It always felt special when I turned from stone back into a boy. Playing War was like that too—I loved how it felt to wake up from being dead, dust off the dirt and leaves, and start the next round of the game.

Jimmy in the back seat of our car.

Baseball

I LOVED BASEBALL almost as much as War. I played pickup games all over the neighborhood. Even when my friends weren't around, there were always enough kids in my family to form two teams. Many summer nights we played baseball for hours until finally Mom yelled from the house, "It's too dark. You can't even see the ball! Someone's going to get hurt!"

We'd insist we could see the ball fine, but she'd make us come inside.

When I joined a Little League team, Dad signed Jimmy up for the team too. I enjoyed everything about baseball—the rules, coach's signals, equipment, uniforms—but the game bored the heck out of my brother. The coach stuck him in right field, where he passed the time staring up at the sky or looking for bugs in the grass at his feet.

One time a batter hit a solid line drive right at him. But Jimmy wasn't paying attention. He was on his knees, digging for worms, or maybe ants.

"*Fletcher!*" the coach screamed.

Still kneeling, Jimmy looked up, calmly stuck out his glove, and caught the ball. Our team erupted in cheers. Jimmy grinned as if he had planned the whole stunt.

Summer meant baseball, but for me it meant hay fever too. As the baseball rolled through the grass, it picked up pollen, which got on my hands when I picked it up, which got in my eyes when I touched them, which made them start to itch . . .

When I rubbed my eyes the itching got worse and worse. By the end of one Little League game my eyes were nearly swollen shut.

Only Mom knew how to interrupt this cycle before I managed to tear my eyes from their sockets. She would bring me into the house and make me lie down on the couch. Then she'd fold a wet face cloth until it was two inches wide and place it over my tortured eyes.

There was one good thing about being stuck inside on a summer day—Mom would turn the TV to the Red Sox game. The Boston Red Sox were my team, even though they weren't very good. They usually finished in sixth or seventh place, but I didn't care. They were my team, big leaguers who played at Fenway Park in Boston.

Lying in darkness with the wet cloth over my eyes, I could clearly picture the players on the field, the Green Monster, the four white bases on the brown infield. Curt Gowdy, the Red Sox announcer, described the game inning by inning. The Red Sox may not have been the best team, but it seemed to me that our players had the most terrific names: Pumpsie Green, Carl Yastrzemski, Felix Mantilla, Bill Monbouquette. Some afternoons I lay on the couch with that wet face cloth soothing my inflamed eyes, softly repeating *Bill Monbouquette* over and over, just because I loved the sound of that name.

My fourth-grade class picture. I'm in the top row, second from right, with Steve Fishman to my left. Andy Hunt is seated, bottom right.

Michele-with-One-L

FOR ONCE, Mom told me before I heard it from Karen Aaronburg. She was going to have another baby.

"This is it, the last puppy," she promised. Eight kids + two parents = ten Fletchers, which sounded like a nice round number to me.

"Really?" Lainie asked Mom.

"Really," Mom said, stroking my sister's hair. "And I really think this one will be a girl."

"I don't believe it," Lainie replied, folding her arms.

Jimmy and I went to Uncle Paul and Aunt Louise's house in Rhode Island. While I was there I met a girl named Michele, who was about my age. Michele lived two houses away from Louise and Paul. She wasn't my cousin, but she might as well have been, because she was over their house all day, every day. When we got into the station wagon to go to the beach, Michele piled in with us. She'd be there to eat a Popsicle or a grilled hot dog or a fat slice of watermelon with everyone else.

"Do you know how to spell my name?" she asked me one night. A bunch of us had been playing Monopoly outside on the porch.

"Sure." I printed the letters M-I-C-H-E-L-L-E on some paper.

"Wrongo. Look." She took the pencil from me and underlined the H-E-L-L part of what I'd written. "When I was born my mom said, 'There will be no *hell* in my Michele.' Get it? That's why my name's spelled with only one *L*." She bent forward and carefully erased one of the *L*s.

The thing is, her mother's plan didn't work. There *was* hell in Michele, lots of it. She was wilder than any of us. At the beach she swam far out, wriggled out of her bathing suit, and tossed it into the air. At Brooms, she stole wax lips and chocolate cigarettes. She knew all kinds of swears and dirty jokes, but she said them so cheerfully it always made me laugh.

One rainy afternoon we were sitting around at Michele's house, bored stiff.

"Let's play Mass," she suggested.

"Okay," my cousin Paul agreed. "I'll be the priest."

"*I'm* the priest," Michele told him.

The boys snorted at that.

"You're a girl!" Jimmy told her. "You can be a nun."

"I'm not going to be a nun," Michele replied calmly. "It was my idea. Plus, I've got Necco wafers for Communion."

That shut everyone up. We ran down to the basement, and the Mass began. At first Michele tried to lead everyone in a church song, but nobody knew the words. My cousin Chris jumped up and started fake-praying in pig Latin, "Ee-way, ank-thay, od-gay . . ."

Michele didn't appreciate everybody goofing around.

"Shut up!" she yelled, holding up the pack of Necco wafers. "Line up if you want to receive Holy Communion!"

My cousin Donna was first in line. She knelt down so Michele could put a white wafer onto her pink tongue. Suddenly we heard a yell from upstairs.

"Ice cream truck!"

Everybody bolted for the stairs. I started to leave, but Michele grabbed my arm. She held out a Necco wafer, a brown one, my favorite.

"Don't you want to receive Communion?" she asked.

"Okay, okay." I did want that brown Necco

wafer, but I didn't want to miss the ice cream truck, either.

"Kneel down," she said softly. "Close your eyes."

I did, but before I could even stick out my tongue, Michele kissed me on the mouth. Then she ran upstairs, laughing.

Later the rain finally stopped, and we had a big game of Hide-and-Seek. Michele and I hid together in a tree. We waited for a long time but nobody found us, or maybe the game was over. Finally, just to see what would happen, I leaned over and kissed her, the first time I'd ever kissed a girl. I had to hide a shiver of excitement at how soft her lips were and the way they fastened themselves to mine.

Next day, Jimmy and I went back home. We ran into the house and found Mom sitting on the sofa. Lainie was next to her, beaming, holding a baby girl! Kathleen Jean Fletcher. I couldn't remember if I'd ever seen a baby girl before and bent forward to take a closer look. Now we had six boys and two girls.

I went back to life in Marshfield with my family and friends. In September, when school started, Karen Aaronburg gave me one of her looks, like she knew every secret in the entire world. But this time I looked straight back at her, because I had a secret too.

Tommy's third-grade picture.

Rhode Island Reds
Age 12

ONE AFTERNOON Mom took a nap with Joey and Kathy, the baby. Dad wanted to keep the house quiet, so he took the rest of us shopping at a department store. When we walked in I noticed a big commotion in one corner—lots of people, noise, and excitement. We walked over to check it out.

Baby chicks! There must have been hundreds of them, little fur balls peep-peep-peeping like crazy in a long, low cage. What a racket!

"They're so adorable!" Lainie said, kneeling down. The chicks were a rusty red color, scurrying this way and that, falling over each other, one cuter than the next. Dad talked to the man who seemed to be in charge.

"What kind are they?"

"These are Rhode Island Reds," the man explained. "It's an exceptional breed, very high-class chickens."

"I'll have to take your word for it," Dad said, smiling.

"Can we buy one, Dad?" Jimmy asked.

"I guess so," Dad replied.

"We can?" I asked. I stared at my brother and he stared back, both of us unable to believe what we'd just heard.

"Really, Dad?" Lainie asked.

"Sure, why not," Dad said, smiling.

"Can I pick it out?" Tommy asked.

"No fair! Let me pick it!"

"How about you each pick one," Dad suggested.

Each? Our eyes popped open wide. Six chicks! I still couldn't believe it but, before Dad could change his mind, we each quickly told the man which one we wanted. He scooped up the chicks one after another and put them into a small cardboard box.

"That'll be three bucks," the man told Dad. "Bag of chicken feed goes another two bucks."

Dad handed him a five. I thought the price was amazingly cheap. Since I was the oldest, Dad let me carry the chicks out to the car. Everybody kept pushing, trying to peek into the box, talking at the same time.

"Quiet!" Lainie said. "You'll make them nervous!"

"What are you—their mother?" Jimmy demanded.

"They're just babies," Lainie shot back. "They're scared."

When we got home we ran into the kitchen, eager to show Mom. She'd just woken up from her nap, and she still looked groggy.

"Baby chicks?" She stared at Dad. "Have you lost your mind?"

He smiled at her. "Baby chicks grow into hens.

Have you ever eaten a fresh egg? Not store-bought. Fresh."

"I don't believe I have." Mom still wasn't smiling.

"They're delicious," he told her. "In a few months we'll be eating fresh eggs every morning!"

"Yes, and no doubt a few of them will start laying golden eggs," Mom replied with a pretend smile.

We each named our chicks. I called mine Sunshine. Tommy named his Goldie. He really loved Goldie and kept picking her up, cuddling her, and petting her downy back. But the next morning we found Goldie lying on her side, peeping weakly.

"What's wrong?" Tommy asked fearfully.

"I'm not sure," Mom said in a gentle voice, "but it's possible that you squeezed Goldie too hard and broke her neck."

"You killed it," Jimmy told him.

"I did not!" Tommy yelled back.

"Shh," Mom told Jimmy. "We don't know for sure what happened."

"I don't want Goldie to die!" Tommy said, bursting into tears. But there wasn't much we could do. Dad put some chicken feed in the box. Goldie looked up at that mountain of food, but she was too weak to eat.

Goldie died. We buried her in the backyard, on the other side of the stream.

"I want Goldie! I want Goldie!" Tommy kept saying. "Now I don't have no baby chick!"

"You don't have *any* baby chick," Mom corrected him.

"That's what I just said!" Tommy couldn't stop crying. And I couldn't stand to hear one of my brothers or sisters bawling like that.

"Stop crying!" I told him.

"But Goldie's dead!"

"Look, you can share my chick with me, okay?" I offered. "Sunshine is nice."

"Really?" Tommy said, brightening a little. Mom gave him a tissue so he could blow his nose.

"But you can't squeeze its neck," I told him. "Promise?"

"I promise," Tommy said, wiping his nose.

"And when she starts laying eggs," I said, "you can't squeeze the eggs or they'll break."

"I won't," Tommy promised.

"You've got to be gentle."

"Gentle," Tommy repeated, though I seriously doubted he understood the meaning of that word.

Lainie's fourth-grade picture.

Fresh Eggs

THE FIVE REMAINING chicks grew fast. They gobbled up the bag of chicken feed in less than two weeks, and Dad had to go back for another bag, and another right after that. As the chicks got older, their looks changed. They weren't quite so round and fuzzy anymore, but what they lost in cuteness they gained in spunk. Pretty soon they could hop out of their box and run around the backyard. They'd stay in a group, walking around, pecking at seeds, ants, and spiders.

The chicks stayed outside most of the time now, even at night. The way they looked, all wide-eyed and alert, made it seem like they were thinking hard about something (even though Jimmy insisted that their brains were too tiny to think very much). They would have been good pets except for one problem: They pooped all over the place! I tried to avoid stepping in it, but you couldn't always see it on the grass. The poop got on our shoes, and we tracked it into the house, staining the rugs and stairs and making everything stink to the high heavens. Mom went absolutely nuts.

"Take off those shoes! Leave them outside! Do *you* want to clean up this stuff? I never, *ever* should have taken those chicks into the house in the first place."

"Easy," Dad said, helping her clean up the mess. "Remember: Fresh eggs are coming."

"I'm about to come unglued," she shot back.

Early one Saturday morning I heard something outside my window, a sound that was strangely familiar. When I rushed into the kitchen I heard it again. Cockle-doodle-doo! Some of the other kids ran into the kitchen too. Dad stumbled in, half asleep.

"What time is it?" he asked, peering at the clock. Five-fifteen a.m.

"Hey Dad—they're roosters!" Jimmy said, laughing.

"Roosters!" Dad went to the window, looking out into the thin morning light. "Are you sure?"

"Yeah, I just watched them crowing," Jimmy said. "Look! They're all doing it!"

We pressed our faces to the windows in the direction of the backyard. Sure enough, they were all cock-a-doodle-dooing.

"Roosters! Roosters!" Jimmy, Tommy, and I started jumping around, screaming with laughter. The little kids looked confused.

"Roosters are boy chickens," Lainie explained. "They don't lay eggs—only hens do."

"They're not going to be hens?" Bobby asked.

"Nope."

Right then Mom walked into the kitchen, carrying Kathy.

"They're roosters, Mom!" I told her.

Mom stared at Dad.

"Fresh eggs," she said to him. "Isn't that what you promised? Isn't that what you said? It looks like we'll be waiting a long time for those eggs."

Lainie and I giggled.

"I'm sorry," Dad said. He looked sort of dazed. "I had no idea they were roosters. I mean, the man never told us that. Did he, Lainie?"

"Nope." She shook her head. "Guess I'll have to change Jasmine's name to a boy name."

The sound was loud and shrill. Cockle-doodle-doo!

"The neighbors will love this," Dad muttered.

"Just what this family needs," Mom said, looking down at Kathy. "Five more boys in the house!"

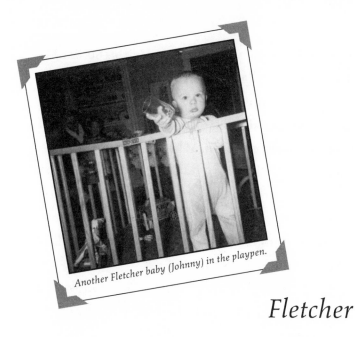

Another Fletcher baby (Johnny) in the playpen.

Fletcher

JIMMY WANTED a hunting crossbow. There was no way Dad would let him get one, so Jimmy had to settle for a bow, but it wasn't a toy. It was a real bow with heavy string and pointed arrows that could pierce the bark of a tree. In the garage, Dad helped him string it.

"Your ancestors were English bow makers," Dad said. "The Fletchers who lived a long time ago. See this part of the arrow with the feathers on it? That's called the fletching."

"Yeah," Jimmy said, running his hand down the smooth fiberglass bow. He was barely listening—the only thing he cared about was getting to shoot. But first Dad had to repeat, for the tenth time, his safety lecture. *A bow and arrow is a deadly weapon. Don't ever point the arrow at anybody. Shoot only at the target. Stand back when somebody is shooting.*

"Okay, okay," Jimmy replied. Dad followed us into the backyard, where he had draped a plastic target over a bale of hay. Jimmy pulled back the bowstring, released the first arrow, and it hit— THWOCK!—the outer ring of the target.

"Good shot," Dad said. "Okay, have fun. Just be careful."

"We will," Jimmy promised.

The moment Dad went inside, Jimmy turned to look at me.

"Watch this," he said.

Before I could say a word, Jimmy had fitted an

arrow into the string, pulled it back, and shot it straight up. The arrow flew like a rocket until I could see nothing but a dot, a point of light, glinting at the top of the sky. But a second later the arrow looked bigger—it was coming down!

"Look out!" Jimmy yelled. We both scrambled to get out of the way, but I hesitated, not sure which way to go. I guessed: right. The arrow brushed past my ear and embedded itself in the ground less than one inch from my sneaker.

"That was close!" I said.

"Hey!" Dad came down the back steps, practically running toward us. From the angry look on his face, I knew he had seen the whole thing. He grabbed the bow from Jimmy and sent us both to our bedroom for the rest of the day.

That night I laid awake in bed, reliving my close escape. When that arrow brushed past my ear it made a soft hissing sound, as if my ancestors were trying to whisper to me.

Jimmy with Kathy.

Tripods

DAD PAID A MAN to clear the acre of woods right behind our house. On Saturday morning we watched him bulldoze bushes and trees. When he had finished, there was a stack of pine logs, each about thirty feet long, and six inches wide at the thickest point, piled at one side of the clearing.

The logs gave Jimmy an idea. He asked me and Tommy to help him carry nine of them to the middle of the clearing.

"Put them in threes," Jimmy said. He directed us to lay the logs so they fit together.

Andy came over from next door. "What are you doing?" he asked.

"You'll see." Jimmy took some twine and started working on a knot at the middle place where the three logs overlapped, like this:

"You know how to tie them together?" I asked.

"I'm going to use a lash knot," Jimmy replied.

"It's too loose."

"No, it's not," Jimmy said. He finished lashing the logs together and stood up. "Now we're going to lift 'em, but we can't do it by ourselves. We're going to need a lot of kids."

"I'll help!" Bobby offered.

"Okay," Jimmy said with a laugh. "But we need some big kids too."

Pretty soon my friends Steve and Larry showed

up. Lee Parker, who was already in junior high, came over too. Jimmy wasted no time putting them to work.

"We'll need two kids on each log," he said. "Ralph and Larry, you guys lift the middle. Everybody ready?"

"Yeah!"

"Okay, lift!"

Larry and I got in the middle and began to lift. As we did, the three-legged thingamajig began to rise from the ground. Jimmy was right about the rope— the knot tightened as the middle part went higher.

"C'mon!" Jimmy yelled. "Push! Lift!"

Up! Up! Sweating, gasping, grunting, we lifted the logs.

Pretty soon the middle part was over our heads and we couldn't reach it anymore. Larry got a long two-by-four and used that to keep pushing it skyward.

"That's good!" Jimmy cried. "That's high enough!"

Everybody cheered. I wiped sweat from my face

and looked up. The top of the tripod stood about twenty-five feet off the ground. But we didn't have any time to rest.

"Two more to go!" Jimmy yelled, and we started erecting the second tripod. On this one he added an extra rope when he lashed the logs together. When we got the structure into place, the rope hung down from the middle. Tommy grabbed the rope and swung back and forth.

"My dad's got some extra tires," Larry offered. "For a rope swing."

"We can do that later!" Jimmy yelled. "C'mon, one more to go!"

By the time we had finished we were exhausted, panting like dogs. But we had done it; all three tripods were standing. It was a typical Jimmy stunt—much harder than anything a teacher would ever ask him to do in school. Jimmy would never earn a grade for imagining those tripods, let alone getting them built. But I knew what he'd done, and the other kids did too. In some ways my brother was a genius.

Dad came outside. All the kids kept quiet while he made a careful inspection, slowly walking around the structures, peering up, touching the logs.

"What are they, anyway?" he finally asked.

"Tripods," Jimmy explained.

"Tripods." Dad nodded. "You realize that if they fall apart, and some kid breaks his neck, I'm responsible."

"They won't fall apart," Jimmy said.

Dad pushed one of the logs, but it hardly moved.

"No, I guess they're not going anyplace," he said. "They seem solid."

"They're solid, all right," Jimmy told him.

"What are they . . . for?" Dad asked, smiling.

"I just wanted to build them." Jimmy shrugged. "To see if I could."

Next morning, when I stepped outside, the sight of those huge tripods took me by surprise, even though I'd help build them. They looked so strange, as if creatures from another planet had chosen my backyard, of all places, to land their spaceships.

Lainie in front of our house. It wasn't as big as it looks!

Attack

DAD WAS AWAY on a business trip. It had snowed on and off all day, and it was cold. In the afternoon Mom bundled up the little kids and took everyone food shopping. We came home an hour later and carried all the grocery bags into the kitchen. We had just started to unpack when Lainie came flying in.

"The roosters!" she cried. "They're dead!"

"Dead?!"

Outside, the chicken coop looked like a murder site. The fence smashed in. Ugly blotches of blood all over the snow. We didn't see any rooster bodies, but feathers were scattered everywhere. I stood there, shocked, trying to force icy air into my lungs.

"They were attacked!" I finally croaked.

"My God!" Mom bent to pick up a feather stained with blood.

"What happened?" Bobby and Johnny asked at the same time.

"Lainie, would you please take the little kids inside?" Mom said, moving so she blocked their view of the bloody pen. "I don't want them to see this. Stay with the baby. I'll be right in."

"Okay," Lainie said, biting her lower lip. She led Bobby, John, and Joey into the house.

"Who would do this?" Tommy demanded.

"Probably a fox, or a dog," Jimmy said, pointing. There were footprints in the snow, dozens of them. "Look."

"I'd bet it was a dog," Mom said, jamming her

hands under her armpits for warmth. On her face was a grim expression I'd never seen before. "The Wallaces' dachshund, Buster, has been snooping around here the last few weeks."

"Buster!" Tommy yelled. "I'll bust him!"

"Hey, I'm cold," Mom said, hugging herself. "Let's go inside."

"I'm going to check around the house first," Jimmy told her.

"Me too," I said. We searched behind and under every bush in the front and back yards, looking for the roosters. Nothing. The sun was going down fast, painting the snow blue.

"They're gone," I said inside the kitchen.

"They're dead," Lainie said in a dazed voice. When she said that, Johnny and Joey looked like they were about to cry.

"We don't know that for sure," Mom said. "Some got killed, no doubt. But some could have escaped and still be alive."

"Really?" Something hopeful flickered in Lainie's eyes. "Where?"

"Ale's Woods," Jimmy suggested. "That's

where I'd go. There's plenty of places to hide in there."

"I wish Dad was here," Lainie put in.

"Daddy!" said Kathy.

"Me too," Bobby said, starting to cry. He came over and leaned against Mom.

"Well, he's not," Mom said, wiping Bobby's nose. She took a deep breath. "And it's starting to get dark. So here's what we're going to do. I'll go out into the woods to look for survivors. I feed those roosters every day when you're in school. They know my voice—they'll come to me. You all stay here."

"You better take me with you," Jimmy said. "I know those woods a lot better than you."

"True." Mom looked over at me. "Okay. You and Lainie keep an eye on everyone. And put away the groceries, please."

Mom opened the closet door and took out Dad's winter coat. It was so huge it completely swallowed her. She pulled on boots, gloves, hat, and scarf. Jimmy only put on his coat, and even then Mom had to make him zipper it.

"Wish us luck," she said.

"We don't need luck," Jimmy said, smiling. "We got me!"

"I hope you're right," Mom told him. She pulled open the door and clomped down the back stairs with Jimmy behind her. The rest of us stood at the window, watching them head toward Ale's Woods.

Lainie and I put away the groceries. Then there was nothing to do but sit around the kitchen and wait while the twilight thickened outside.

"Look," Bobby said, pointing outside. A couple of snowflakes brushed against the window.

"Where's Mom?" Joey whispered.

"Don't worry," Lainie told him. "She'll be here soon."

We waited twenty minutes, a half hour. Then it was pretty much dark, and I began to worry. Suddenly Tommy gave a yell.

"Look!"

"I don't see anything," I said, peering out. Two shapes appeared in the darkness. There they were, Mom and Jimmy, trudging across the snowy lawn. I was amazed to see Jimmy walking with his right arm extended, a rooster perched on that arm! Mom had a rooster on one of her arms too.

"Two! They found two!"

They didn't head to the broken chicken pen. Instead, they tromped up the steps and in through the back door without even stopping to shake snow off their boots.

"You did it!"

Everyone cheered.

"Those roosters are heavier than you think!" Mom said, flopping into a chair. The two birds moved excitedly on the linoleum floor and ruffled their feathers, shaking off the cold.

"It's Peepers!" Lainie cried, saying the name of her rooster.

"You can't tell," Jimmy said, pulling off his coat.

"I can so! Look at the white spot on his back feathers! And the other one's yours, Jimmy! It's Stephen!"

"Stephen, really? Well, maybe you're right," Jimmy agreed.

Johnny put some chicken feed on the floor, and the roosters began eagerly pecking it up.

"How'd you find them?" I asked.

"We went way far back in the woods," Mom said. "I kept calling and calling, hoping they'd hear my voice and recognize it."

"Yeah, then we heard a noise, like a squawk," Jimmy explained. "Then I just looked up and saw one—twenty feet up in a tree!"

"I didn't know roosters could fly!" Bobby said, grinning.

"I called a few times, and it flew down to me," Mom explained. "We found the other one about fifty feet away. They looked awful cold and jittery, poor things."

We all agreed: The survivors were Stephen and Peepers. Which meant that my rooster, Sunshine, probably died in the attack. In bed I cried, muffling the sound so Jimmy wouldn't hear. But knowing that Stephen and Peepers had escaped alive softened the ache in my chest.

That night, Mom let Stephen and Peepers sleep

in the basement. Dad came home and rebuilt the chicken coop. He replaced the wooden supports on the fence with a much heavier wood. And he added a hinged top, with a latch that locked.

At school Jimmy bragged about the Great Rooster Rescue in the deepest part of Ale's Woods. But to me, Mom was the real hero of the story. She never gave up on those two roosters. Somehow she had known they would be alive. And she braved darkness, cold, and snow to bring them back.

Jimmy with Lainie.

Tea Rock Lane

"How are your roosters doing?" Freddy Black asked on the bus one day. Freddy was a year younger than me and lived a half mile from our house.

"Okay," I mumbled, which wasn't exactly true. It had been a cold, wet spring. Stephen and Peepers didn't look very happy, shivering in the wire chicken coop Dad had built. I wondered if they missed their brothers.

"My dad said we'll take them," Freddy offered. "If you want."

I looked at him, surprised. "Take them?"

"Yeah, they can come live with us," he said. "We got chickens, you know. We get three dozen eggs every day, sometimes more."

"I don't know."

"Well, think about it," Freddy said.

That night at supper I repeated Freddy's offer. It didn't sound like a bad idea to me, but it was up to Jimmy and Lainie, since Stephen and Peepers belonged to them.

"I'm not sure," Lainie said, chewing her lower lip.

"I know we've been through a lot with those roosters, and we've all grown attached to them," Dad said. "But the truth is, we're not equipped to take care of them properly."

"I still get complaints from the neighbors," Mom said. "Those birds do make an awful racket at five in the morning!"

I realized I'd gotten so used to the sound that I slept right through it.

"If they went to Mr. Black's house they'd be

living with chickens," Dad pointed out, winking. "Girls."

"Dad!" Lainie glared at him.

"What's wrong with that?" Dad replied innocently.

"They do seem kind of lonely," Jimmy agreed. "Yeah, all right. It's okay by me."

"Well, I guess so," Lainie said in a small voice. "I want them to be happy. But I'm going to visit them every week, okay?"

"Okay," Mom promised.

On Friday after school, Mr. Black showed up. He was an all-business kind of guy, not very talkative or smiley, but he seemed to know what he was doing. Working quickly, he caught the roosters, put them into two small carry cages, and drove away. Lainie was crying so hard she wouldn't even come outside to say good-bye.

Next day, Dad and Mom had planned a family trip to an animal farm in New Hampshire. The other kids were excited, but I felt too old for that sort of thing.

"Can I please stay home, Dad?" I asked.

"This is family time," Dad replied.

"I know," I said, "but I've already been to that place at least five times. It's for little kids."

"Me too," Jimmy agreed. "Can we stay home? Please, Dad?"

Dad gave us a long look. "Okay," he finally said. "But I'm trusting you guys to be responsible and stay out of trouble. Promise?"

"Promise," Jimmy said.

"You can make yourselves peanut butter sandwiches for lunch," Mom said. "If there's an emergency, you can always call the Hunts' house."

"I know," I told her.

So they left. In the morning Jimmy went over to Ricky Topham's house. I hung out with Andy until he had to go to the dentist. Then I went home and made myself a sandwich for lunch. It was a little weird being in the house when it was so quiet. Afterward, I decided to take a bike ride, and about a block from my house I spotted Lee Topham, Ricky's big brother, talking with Freddy Black. I rode up to them, eager to hear how Stephen and Peepers were doing in their new home.

"We had a big problem with your roosters," Freddy told me.

"A problem? What do you mean?"

"See, we have these three other roosters?" Freddy said. "And your roosters started a fight with ours. Well, I'm not sure who started it, but anyway it got pretty nasty. There were feathers all over the place. Dad said if there's one more fight . . ." He shook his head sadly.

"What?" I asked.

"Dad said, 'Heads are gonna roll,' " Freddy said. "He's gonna have to kill them."

"Kill them?!"

Freddy nodded. I started to ask which roosters would get killed, but the answer was obvious.

"They're our pets," I said stupidly. The shock was wearing off, and I could feel myself getting hot.

"Yeah, well, your pets almost ripped apart one of our roosters," Freddy replied. "I'm just telling you what happened."

"He better not kill them!" I took a deep breath and tried to calm down. "Is your dad home now?"

"Nope, he and Mom went to Boston," Freddy said. "They won't be back 'til tonight."

I got on my bike and started riding, thinking hard. What to do? I couldn't get in touch with Dad or Mom, and I couldn't talk to Mr. Black until later. What if there was another rooster fight tonight? Was this what Mom meant when she said I could call Mrs. Hunt in case of an emergency?

I needed Jimmy. I rode up and down Acorn Street for twenty minutes and finally found him at Tea Rock Lane, talking with Ricky Topham. Tea Rock Lane was a circular driveway. It had a historical plaque that explained how on this spot the colonists burned British tea before the Revolutionary War. Marshfield had so many historical markers like this we hardly paid attention to them.

"What's up?" Jimmy asked, seeing the look on my face.

I told him what Freddy had told me.

"His father said heads are gonna roll," I said. "He's going to axe them."

Ricky laughed.

Jimmy glared at him. "You ever seen a chicken get his head cut off?" he asked.

"No," Ricky admitted.

"Well, I have," Jimmy said. "It's nasty."

I had too. Two years ago, in Larry Waters's backyard, I watched his big sister kill a chicken with an axe. There was a ton of blood. But the most horrifying thing was when the headless chicken got up and started running around, its legs going like crazy. It ran for fifteen or twenty seconds before it finally keeled over for good.

"Chickens are so stupid," his big sister had said, "it takes 'em a while to realize they're dead." She had laughed at her own joke, but I felt like I was going to be sick.

"What're we going to do?" I asked. "Dad and Mom might not get home 'til seven or eight."

"That could be too late," Jimmy said. "C'mon. We've got to go get them."

"How?"

"We've got to take them," Jimmy said.

"You mean, like, kidnap them?" I asked.

"Rescue them."

"We can't just walk into their yard when they're not home," I objected. "That's against the law."

Jimmy rolled his eyes and swore loudly.

"Well, it is," I insisted. "It's trespassing."

"Do you want to keep those roosters alive, or not? Who *cares* if it's trespassing?" Jimmy pointed at the historical plaque for Tea Rock Lane. "You think the colonists worried about breaking the law when they burned that tea? Or when they dumped it in Boston Harbor? They did it because it was the right thing to do."

The whole time Jimmy was talking, I had Dad's words—*I'm trusting you guys to be responsible and stay out of trouble*—buzzing around in my head. But I realized that my brother had a point.

"I'm going to get them," Jimmy announced.

"Count me in," Ricky said.

Jimmy looked at me. "You coming, or not?"

"All right," I finally said.

The three of us got on our bikes and rode as fast as we could to Freddy Black's house. When we got there, I was relieved that there wasn't a car in the driveway.

"Think Freddy's home?" Jimmy asked.

"I hope not," I said, glancing at the house. It felt funny to be talking in a whisper in the middle of the day. "Let's just do it and get the heck out of here."

We had to climb a wire fence to get into the yard. The chickens watched us suspiciously. We spotted Stephen and Peepers, but if they recognized us they sure didn't show it. Jimmy ducked into the chicken house and came out with the two small cages Mr. Black had used.

"Here, Stephen," I said, taking a step forward, but the rooster backed away. Jimmy tossed down a handful of feed. When Stephen scurried in to eat with the other chickens, I grabbed him by the feet. He started squawking furiously, flapping his wings, but I managed to get him into the cage and slam the door shut before he could peck me in the face. We did the same with Peepers.

"Let's go!" I said nervously. Ricky climbed over

the fence first, and we handed the cages over to him. Then we got on our bikes and started for home, Jimmy holding one cage, me holding the other. It was hard to ride like that, balancing the heavy cage on my lap. Peepers was upset and kept shifting his weight from one side of the cage to the other.

I kept expecting to see a police car or to hear someone yell at us. But as we drove down the street, cars passed us like it was the most normal thing in the world to see two kids biking along with caged roosters perched on their handlebars. Sweat was running down my back by the time we finally got to our house. When we opened the cages, Stephen and Peepers burst out, ruffling their feathers and giving us the evil eye from inside our chicken coop.

"You'll appreciate this someday," I said, laughing because I knew they never would.

Then we waited. Jimmy and I stayed inside watching TV. I felt half-scared, half-excited at what we'd done.

The phone rang, and I jumped up to answer it.

"Don't!" Jimmy said. "It could be Mr. Black!"

"It could be Dad or Mom," I replied, but I let the phone ring until it finally stopped.

At six forty-five Dad and Mom came home. The little kids must've seen the roosters in the backyard because they came running inside, all excited.

"Stephen and Peepers!" Tommy cried.

"They're home!" Johnny yelled.

Mom just stared at us. She didn't exactly look happy.

"What happened?" Lainie asked.

"They flew the coop," Jimmy said, but I shot him a look. This was the wrong time to act like a wise guy.

"What happened?" Dad asked again.

So I explained everything. He listened without interrupting.

"Going onto someone's property and taking something when they're not there, that's serious business," Dad pointed out.

"I know, Dad," I admitted. "But we didn't know when you'd be home."

"They're not somebody's property—they're our pets!" Lainie cried.

"But we gave them to Mr. Black," Mom reminded her. "They're his responsibility now."

"Yeah," Jimmy said, "but we had to rescue them or they would've been decapitated! He was gonna kill them!"

"I'd better give Mr. Black a call," Dad said. He went upstairs to use the phone. It must have been a short conversation, because he came down two minutes later.

"Well, I talked with him," Dad said.

"Was he mad?" I asked.

"Not after I explained why you guys did it," Dad said. "He said that roosters are very territorial. And it sounds like his roosters and ours didn't exactly hit it off. We both agreed that it might be better if Stephen and Peepers stay here."

"Yes!" the kids all cheered.

"I knew it was too good to last," Mom said with a sigh.

"At least they're away from those mean old roosters," Lainie said. "I'm glad they're home."

"Temporarily," Dad corrected her. Then he looked at Mom and winked at her. "We're still going to find a better place for them to live. Everything will work out fine."

But Mom didn't look convinced.

"Ever since you brought those cute little chicks into this house," she told Dad, *"nothing* has turned out the way you said it would!"

Top row: Jimmy, me, Lainie, and Tommy; bottom row: Johnny, Bobby, Joey, and Kathy.

The First Team
Age 13

IT HAPPENED ON the next-to-last day of school. Karen Aaronburg turned and gave me a sly smile.

"Have you heard the scuttlebutt?" she asked.

I made a face at her. "My mom's not having a baby," I told her.

"True." She nodded. "But I heard something even more important."

I tried not to care, but she had hooked me, again.

"About . . . me?" I asked.

She nodded.

"What?"

"You're moving," Karen said.

"No way," I told her.

She nodded. "Ask your parents."

I wanted to believe she was lying, except for one thing: Karen was always right. The teacher was talking about active verbs and passive verbs, but I couldn't concentrate. Moving? After school I jumped off the bus and ran into the house.

"Are we moving?" I demanded.

Mom looked guilty. "How did you—," she began.

"Karen Aaronburg!" I interrupted. "Well, are we?"

"Yes," Mom admitted. "I'm sorry you didn't hear it from us first. We're moving to Chicago."

"Chicago?" I'd seen the city on a map of the United States. "Why there?"

"That's where the regional office for Dad's work is," Mom said. "He's getting a big promotion."

◆ ◆ ◆

After supper I walked outside and sat on the boulder in the front yard. It was my favorite place, my thinking rock, but my head was still swirling and I couldn't think. *Moving.* I was glad my best friend Andy Hunt wasn't outside. I'd have to tell him, and I didn't want to say that awful word out loud.

Dad always got home from work after we ate supper. Now he came outside and stood beside me. "I guess you heard the news."

"Yeah." I didn't look at him.

"You okay?" he asked.

I said nothing.

"I remember when you were little," he said. "You used to play Statue on this rock. You sure loved that game."

He smiled, but in my head I pictured another kid, a stranger, sitting on my rock after I was gone to Chicago. Not a pretty picture.

"Why do we have to move?" I demanded. "You've got a good job here, don't you?"

"I do," Dad said. "But in my business, Boston is

the second team. Chicago is where the real action is. All my life I've wanted to play on the first team, and now I've got the chance. I'm excited about that. Maybe someday you'll understand the feeling."

Dad went into the house. I felt too agitated to go inside, so I started wandering down Acorn Street. The night air was warm and school was just about over, but the idea of summer left me cold. I stopped by another boulder, this one at the edge of Ale's Woods. When I was in first grade, my brother Jimmy found three long fluorescent bulbs someone had put out with the trash, and smashed them against this granite boulder. Then we heard that fluorescent bulbs were filled with poisonous gas. After that, whenever we ran past this rock we held our breath. I realized I was doing that now—six years later, I was still holding my breath.

All my life, Dad said, *I've wanted to play on the first team, and now I've got the chance.*

What did he mean by that? I had spent my

whole life living on Acorn Street. This neighbor-hood felt like my bones, my skin. I thought of Ale's Woods, our woods, Mud Puppy Place. I thought of my three best friends—Andy Hunt, Steve Fishman, Larry Waters. I thought of Jimmy Dean, Ricky and Lee Topham, Timmy Ross, Freddy Black, Sophie and Arthur Pratt, and so many others. The first team? How could this not be the first team?

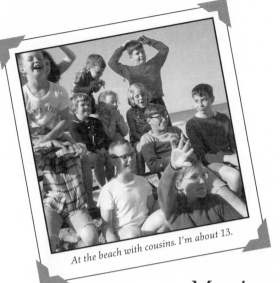
At the beach with cousins. I'm about 13.

Moving Days

Nobody was happy about moving, except maybe Mom and Dad, and the little kids, who didn't really have a clue what "moving" meant.

"Chicago's not near the ocean," Lainie pointed out one night at supper.

Jimmy moaned. "No geography lesson, okay?"

"No, but it's on Lake Michigan, which is huge," Dad said. "When you're on the lake, you can't see the other side. It's like being at the ocean, except it's fresh water, not salt."

"I don't want to move," Tommy said. He stuck out his lower lip and folded his arms across his chest.

"Me neither," Jimmy agreed.

"Are Stephen and Peepers coming with us?" Johnny asked.

"No," Mom said, shaking her head. "We'll find a good home for them here in Marshfield."

"Am I gonna move?" Bobby asked, looking up at Mom.

"No, you've got to stay here," Jimmy told him. Bobby's face fell. It looked like he was going to cry.

"That was so mean," Lainie said, glaring at him.

"So what?" Jimmy made a face at her.

"Jimmy." Mom gave him a warning look.

"Hey, I was just kidding!" Jimmy replied, looking at Bobby. "Can't you take a joke?"

Bobby nodded his head and tried to smile.

"You're definitely coming with us," Mom said,

rubbing the top of Bobby's head. "How could we go anywhere without you?"

Mom and Dad stayed busy packing, but Jimmy made himself scarce. I got glimpses of him wandering through the woods, alone or with his friend Ricky. Once, I saw him near a stone wall, at a place where we often dug up colorful glass bottles among the trash that someone had buried long ago.

We made our final trip to Rexhame Beach. Jimmy found a dead sand shark that had washed up on shore. He ran back to our blanket to get his pocket knife. The kids who gathered to watch squealed when they saw Jimmy cut open the shark's belly. He located the shark's stomach and sliced that open too. One girl gagged and ran off.

"You can see what he ate before he died," Jimmy said, showing us a bottle cap plus two small, partly digested fish.

That night I listened to Jimmy breathing in his bed. Roaming around outside was what he loved best, and the idea of moving away from the woods must have been terrifying for him. But he didn't talk about it, so I could only guess. I worried about him; he still wasn't doing very well in school. Would things be any different in Illinois?

The next day I wanted to have one final game of War, and so I took it upon myself to organize a big one with all my brothers and friends and the neighborhood kids. My team had my brothers plus Andy, Steve, and Larry. It was our best War ever, and it ended with a bloody battle, everybody standing twenty feet away from each other, holding up their sticks and firing at point-blank range. Then the last kid fell and the woods went quiet. I didn't want the game to end, so I lay there for a whole minute, letting imaginary smoke drift away in the breeze.

Mom stood on a chair and wiped my fingerprints off the doorjamb for the last time. She packed dozens and dozens of boxes, but for some reason I still found it hard to wrap my head around the word: *moving*. I had lived in that house in Marshfield practically my whole life, and it never occurred to me that we might end up living anywhere else. I figured I had a lock on this place, that I'd be here forever, or at least until I grew up, the way Karen Aaronburg knew she would be sitting in the first seat, first row, at school until she graduated from high school.

Mom brought the electric clippers outside and gave each boy a whiffle haircut. I went last, and by then there were clumps of hair all over the porch. Mom always told us that birds would add our cut hair to twigs and grass to make their nests. That had sounded like a fairy tale, but now I wanted to believe that some part of me might live on in these woods after I was gone.

"Nice haircuts," Dad said at supper.

I looked down the table at Jimmy, Tommy, Bobby, Johnny, and Joey. Mom had cut our hair extra-short; my brothers reminded me of the baby chicks when we first got them. I must've looked that way too.

"Who wants another slice?" Mom asked. All

the silverware had been packed away, so we were eating pizza on paper plates. Mrs. Pratt had brought over the pizza, a salad, some chips, and guacamole, which we hardly ever ate.

"I do," Tommy said.

"I don't!" Kathy said. A three-year-old, she spoke with a funny, high-pitched voice.

"How's everybody doing?" Dad asked, as if he didn't know. We were all feeling pretty glum. "Jimmy?"

"One thing you never told me," Jimmy said. "Do they have any woods near our new house?"

"I don't know for sure," Dad said. "I saw lots of trees."

"Trees aren't woods," Jimmy pointed out.

"My friends won't be there," Lainie murmured.

"But don't forget," Mom said. "All ten of us will be moving."

Jimmy leaned back and noisily cracked his knuckles. "Unfortunately," he sighed.

"That's not a bad thing," Mom told him. "You'll be in a new neighborhood, but you'll already have eight kids to play with."

I'd never thought of it that way before. On the first day we could play a game of War—me, Bobby, and Joey versus Jimmy, Tommy, and Johnny. It wouldn't be the same without Andy, Steve, and Larry, not nearly, but I told myself it was better than nothing.

"Who wants some guacamole?" Mom asked.

"I do," Dad said.

"Yuck!" said Kathy, pointing at the greenish goop.

"You should try it," Mom said to her. "It's really good."

"I *don't* want rock 'n rolly!" Kathy cried, which cracked everybody up.

We still didn't have a place for Stephen and Peepers. Finally, Mr. Waters, Larry's father, said they could come live with them.

"We've got hens but no roosters," he said, "so there shouldn't be any fighting like there was at the other place."

It seemed like the perfect solution, given the fact that there was no way Mom would let us bring the roosters to Illinois. Mr. Waters was a nice guy, and I just knew he wouldn't get rid of our roosters the first time they got into trouble. So we agreed. Mr. Waters came over with his pickup truck early one morning and took the roosters away.

Next day, the whole family went over to Larry's house to check on them. The roosters ignored us, but it was hard to feel sad with Stephen and Peepers looking so happy in their new home. The birds strutted around like a couple of VIPs, heads high, chests out, surrounded by four dozen clucking hens.

"They've always had lots of attitude," Mom said, laughing.

"That's a good thing for a rooster to have," Mr. Waters replied.

"We're gonna move, but they moved first," Bobby whispered.

"We won't be able to check on them when we're in Illinois," Lainie said sadly.

"Don't worry," Dad told her. "Look at the nice big yard they've got to play in."

"And there's a snug henhouse for cold nights," Mr. Waters said. "Believe me, your roosters got it made in the shade."

I nodded. I believed that Stephen and Peepers would be fine in their new home. I just wished I could be sure that the same would be true for me.

Aunt Mary is holding Kathy at a final dinner with Mom, Dad, me, and Joey.

The Last Night

AFTER SUPPER I went outside. It was late July, still light at seven o'clock, one of those summer days that felt like it would go on forever, except I knew it would end. There was no way around it. Tomorrow we'd get in the car and start driving west toward Chicago.

In the clearing, I walked under the tripods that Jimmy designed and we built two years ago.

175

What would the people who were buying our house do with these gangly wooden structures? Leave them? Tear them down? It made me sad to think about it.

I spotted a cluster of lady slippers. I thought of these wildflowers as royalty, the queens of the plant world. They were endangered—you could get a fifty-dollar fine for digging one up. I always felt rich with those expensive ladies growing wild in our woods, until now.

I wished Andy would come outside. He'd been staying away for the past few days. So had Larry and Steve. I needed to talk to those guys. I missed them a lot, and I hadn't even left yet.

That night I laid in bed, hearing the songs of the crickets and feeling miserable. The door opened. Dad walked in. When he saw that Jimmy was asleep, he came and sat on my bed.

"Can't sleep?" he asked softly.

"Nope."

"A lot's going on," he said. "Tomorrow's the big day."

I turned toward the wall.

"I know this has been hard for you." He put his hand on my shoulder. "But you'll see, Ralph. It's going to be all right."

For a crazy second I imagined him saying, *I changed my mind. We're not going to move.*

Of course, that didn't happen. But what did was just as amazing. He leaned down and kissed me on the forehead, something he hadn't done since I was a little kid.

That night I had a dream about Great Grandma. She died a few years ago, but in the dream she was in the backyard, wearing her favorite gray sweatshirt, and I was there too. We were standing beside the garden, at the spot where I once saw her plant some of our teeth.

"It didn't work," I said. "Look. Nothing ever grew here."

"That's not true," she replied, smiling. "Look at your arms and those two long legs. Something did grow in this place—that something is you!"

And that made me feel better.

Me, holding a garden hose.

Funeral

ON OUR LAST MORNING in Marshfield the door-bell rang at nine o'clock. When I opened it I saw Andy, Steve, and Larry standing together. I was surprised to see them.

"C'mon, we're taking you to the woods," Larry said.

Dad came downstairs carrying two suitcases.

"Can I go into the woods?" I asked Dad.

He shook his head. "We're leaving in less than an hour."

"Please, Dad," I pleaded. "Just one last time?"

"All right, but we're leaving at ten o'clock sharp," he said. "When you hear me beep the horn, you come right away, okay?"

"Okay," I promised, and followed my friends outside. They were walking in a funny way, the way you do when you're hiding a secret.

"What's going on?" I asked.

"We're having a funeral," Andy replied with a solemn face.

"For who?"

"You," Steve explained.

"A funeral!" I laughed. "Hey, I'm moving. I'm not dead!"

"You'll be dead to us," Larry pointed out.

We entered Ale's Woods on a path I'd run down thousands of times. I knew every rock and mushroom and pine tree by heart. In the middle of the woods my friends stopped.

"There!" Steve said, pointing to a small indentation in the forest floor. "Lie down, dead man!"

I lay down. The ground was thick with pine needles, and soft. My friends picked up big clumps of pine needles and started sprinkling them over my body.

"Hey!" I protested.

"Be quiet," Larry ordered. "You're dead, remember? Keep your eyes closed."

"Just don't get it on my face," I muttered. They kept sprinkling the pine needles on me until my limbs and body were covered, and I could feel them, like a lightweight blanket.

"Should auld acquaintance be forgot—," Steve sang.

"You don't sing that at a funeral," Larry interrupted. "You sing that on New Year's Eve!"

Andy loudly cleared his throat. "Hear ye, hear ye, hear ye," he announced. "We have gathered here to lay to rest the soul of our departed friend, Ralph Fletcher. Would anyone like to speak?"

"I would," Steve said. "Ralph Fletcher was a good friend. Last year I had to do summer school. He came by every day to walk me home."

"He was a good friend," Larry agreed. "About a

month ago, John Berkowitz tried to beat me up, and Ralph told John, 'You'll have to beat me up first.' So, John Berkowitz punched him instead. He was a brave friend. Stupid, but brave!"

Everyone laughed, including me.

"He was a good friend," Andy began, then stopped. I lay on the pine needles, eyes shut, smelling the mix of the piney smell and the good, rotting earth underneath. I waited for Andy to continue, but he didn't say anything. Then he whispered:

"He was the brother I never had."

"He was a member of the Four Stooges," Larry said in a husky whisper. Then they all said together:

"We'll never forget him."

My eyes started to water. I tilted my head so they wouldn't notice, and stayed quiet. Nobody spoke. I thought of all the things I'd done with these guys. Staying up late listening to the radio while the DJ counted down the top ten. Blowing off M-80s in Mr. Oxner's cornfield. Eating raw sweet corn. Going to the Marshfield Fair every summer. Arguing about which girl in our class was cuter—Lisa Kennedy, Pam Coyne, or Beth Byers. Fishing for crappies and sunfish. Trading baseball cards, card tricks, dirty jokes, scars, stories, snacks, swears.

For a long moment it stayed quiet. Finally I opened my eyes.

They were gone.

Usually I hated it when my friends ditched me, but this time it felt different. In a strange way I was glad they were gone. For a while I just laid there, looking up at the trees. I heard a car horn beeping.

"Ralph!" It was Jimmy, calling. "C'mon, we gotta go!"

"Coming!" I yelled back. I sat up and brushed off the pine needles. Bits of light danced in the deep forest shadows around me. I knew I'd never forget that place. Then I stood up and stepped into my new life, whatever that might be.

20352179

921
FLETCHER